PRIDE
AND
PERSEVERANCE
A STORY OF COURAGE, HOPE, AND REDEMPTION

PRIDE AND PERSEVERANCE

A STORY OF COURAGE, HOPE, AND REDEMPTION

Conrad Dobler

TRIUMPH
BOOKS

No part of this publication may be reproduced, stored in a retrieval system, or transmitted in any form by any means, electronic, mechanical, photocopying, or otherwise, without the prior written permission of the publisher, Triumph Books, 542 South Dearborn Street, Suite 750, Chicago, Illinois 60605.

Triumph Books and colophon are registered trademarks of Random House, Inc.

Library of Congress Cataloging-in-Publication Data
Dobler, Conrad.
  Pride and perseverance : a story of courage, hope, and redemption /
Conrad Dobler.
    p. cm.
  ISBN 978-1-60078-298-5
1. Dobler, Conrad. 2. Football players-United States-Biography. 3. People with disabilities-United States-Biography. I. Title.
  GV939.D63A3 2009
  796.332092-dc22
  [B]

                                                          2009030311

This book is available in quantity at special discounts for your group or organization. For further information, contact:

Triumph Books
542 South Dearborn Street
Suite 750
Chicago, Illinois 60605
(312) 939–3330
Fax (312) 663–3557
www.triumphbooks.com

Printed in U.S.A.
ISBN: 978-1-60078-298-5
Design by Sue Knopf
Photos courtesy of the author unless otherwise indicated

To the memory of my father

To my mother and all of my siblings

*To my wife Joy; to my children Mark and his wife Dina,
Erin and her husband Chad, Abbey, Franco, Holli, and
Stephen; and to my grandchildren Jordin, Zane, Matissen,
Kinsington, Brady, and Frances*

*To all those family members, friends, and strangers
who through their random acts of kindness and support
helped my family through difficult times*

*To all of those in the spinal cord injury and
stem cell research community who are working to find a cure*

*To all my retired NFL brothers and their families
who are in crisis and are fighting
for humanitarian support and
the improved benefits that we so desperately need*

*To all of the fans who have followed my career;
you have provided me with much joy and happiness*

*To those who find themselves in the middle of a storm;
I hope that through the experiences
that I have written about in this book
you are inspired to persevere and keep fighting*

CONTENTS

FOREWORD

I have known Conrad Dobler now for almost 40 years, and I truly love the guy. He is just like a brother to me. Although we have not lived in the same city for the last 30 years, there is never a week that goes by when Conrad and I don't talk. He has always been the ultimate teammate, both on and off the field. Of course, we played side by side as teammates for the St. Louis Cardinals in the 1970s and had a remarkable professional relationship in the NFL. We played in tandem, like two parts of a well-running machine. Conrad was the right guard, and I was the right tackle. We were joined at the hip. As I said when I was inducted into the Pro Football Hall of Fame, I would never have made it there without the other guys on the line with me, and Conrad is at the top of that list. Of course, we were different types of players. (I never bit anybody!) Still, we could not possibly have been closer as teammates, and we have remained that close throughout the rest of our lives.

Even though Conrad has this public image of being a real tough guy, you may find it surprising to learn that Conrad is the kind of person who would give you the shirt off his back and would sacrifice his own well-being and happiness to do the right thing to help other people in need. He created this image of himself as "pro football's dirtiest player," and he even reveled in it. It worked for him, and he used it to his advantage. But that image is far from the real Conrad Dobler that I know and love. Especially in recent years, since his wife's life-changing accident, my admiration for Conrad has only continued to grow. There has not been a lot of sunshine in his life since then, and so I have marveled at how—like the little Dutch boy with his thumb in the dike—Conrad has managed to keep everything together. But Conrad has just about run out of fingers. I really feel for Conrad and his family's struggle, for what he must endure each day. But he is the ultimate fighter. He hates to lose and refuses to throw in the towel. Even when they traded him away from St. Louis, when his knees started to go, he continued as a starter for the New Orleans Saints and then again as a starter for the Buffalo Bills.

Now, none of us are perfect, including Conrad. (Believe it or not!) But for all his flaws, I have to say that there is an inherent decency about Conrad that most people would never realize unless they really get to know him. Yes, he's loud and boisterous, and he loves to be the life of the party—and maybe he tells the worst jokes ever! But he is a real man in my book; a first-class individual. I would even go so far as to say that he is a good candidate for sainthood, and I don't know many people like that. Conrad is generous to a fault and has a huge heart. In spite of his own travails, he thinks all the time about helping other people in need, and he has a spiritual side that he does not reveal readily to others. Anyone who thinks that Conrad Dobler is just that guy on the cover of *Sports Illustrated* from 1977 doesn't really know him very well.

Even though Conrad is famous and has lived the dream, excelling as a Pro Bowl–caliber player in the NFL, he is an example to us all that life is a constant struggle and can be full of surprises, even for the mightiest among us. Just because you may have success one day, like playing in the NFL or whatever, that does not give you an automatic guarantee for the future; it does not mean you will be financially or physically set for life. Whether or not you are a football fan, we all have something to learn from the example set by Conrad Dobler. His story is a reminder for us all to keep fighting, especially when things get tough, and to never give up.

—*Dan Dierdorf*

1

GROWING UP TOUGH

*"I thoroughly enjoyed hitting people,
and I couldn't believe
there was actually a sport
that allowed me to take out
my aggression on people.
What a beautiful country."*

My name is Conrad Francis Dobler, and I guess you could say that I have been causing trouble since the day I was brought into this world, back on October 1, 1950, to John and Clara Dobler in Chicago, Illinois. In fact, as soon as my mother went into labor, all hell broke loose!

First, my dad was pulled over and got a traffic ticket on their way to Evangelical Hospital in Chicago. Then, while he was rushing to get my mom inside the emergency room, he fell on the sidewalk and hurt his leg. The nurses saw him limping and immediately came to his aid, figuring he was the one who was in need of medical attention and not my mom.

While the nurses were still attending to my injured dad, my mom had been wheeled into an elevator on a stretcher so that she could be taken up to the delivery room. By that time, I suppose, Mom and I couldn't wait any longer, so out I came—right there on the elevator, in between two floors! There weren't even any doctors or nurses on board either, just a couple of very nervous orderlies. My mom was one tough customer though, so she probably barked out precise instructions for them on exactly what to do.

Actually, to say that my mom was tough would be an understatement. My mother was physically a very, very strong woman. She drove a milk truck while she was pregnant, for Pete's sake! She had that old-country devotion to hard work; that was just how she was wired.

Mom grew up as one of 10 surviving children (two of her siblings had been stillborn). Her parents were Polish immigrants, Ignatius and Victoria Broniecki, and their family lived on the south side of Chicago where my grandmother worked as a cook. Her best customers included none other than the notorious mob boss Al Capone and his cronies, who apparently enjoyed good, authentic Polish food.

Mom was a real control freak, and I definitely got that from her. She was right, even when she was wrong. She was also a little bit eccentric, a born storyteller, and she loved to stretch the truth a little. I definitely got that trait from her as well. You would think she suffered from every sickness known to man, too, which I think was more for sympathy than anything else. For whatever the reason, she just likes drama and kind of enjoyed being the martyr. In her eyes, our family was like *Ozzie and Harriet*, a life full of strawberries and cream. I don't think it was even close to that, but that was how she saw things.

My mom now lives with my sister Corrine in Twentynine Palms, California, in a big new house. Corrine won the California State Lottery several years ago and will collect around $80,000 a year for the next 30 years. I am just happy my mom is being taken care of because that means there is one less thing I need to worry about.

My father grew up in Chicago as well, alongside three brothers and two sisters. His mother was an Irish American girl whose maiden name was Catherine MacIntire, and his father was a German American guy by the name of Fred Dobler. My father was definitely not a touchy-feely kind of a guy. He never grabbed me and said, "Hey son, I love you." That wasn't him at all. Dad was a big, 300-pound, no-nonsense, tough-as-nails kind of a guy. He was a provider, and that was how he showed his love.

My dad was always cursing, too, which is why I have a garbage mouth. Although he never cursed in the house (Mom wouldn't tolerate that, nor was it appropriate around any girls or women), out on the loading docks or in the garage it was "F—" this and "F—" that. My favorite saying of his was when he referred to someone or something as "that rat-eating bastard!" That was just the way he was.

My dad had served in the army during WWII in Northern Africa and Sicily. Even though he was only a cook, he was proud of his service, and he once earned some kind of commendation when a bomb hit an ammunition truck near the mess hall where they had just prepared a meal for the troops. Dad jumped into the burning truck to move it away from the mess tent so the tent wouldn't catch fire. I am sure that he did it so he would not lose all the work they had just done to prepare the meal, but he was recognized by the army for his heroic act. He told me that most heroes are made by circumstances, more so than by acts of courage. He said if he had known that the truck was loaded with ammo he would never have gotten close to it! But he told me that when circumstances place you square in the middle of a situation, you are required as a fellow human being to do the right thing.

After WWII, my dad got a job as a corrections officer in a prison. However, after witnessing a great deal of cruel treatment to several of the inmates, he decided to quit the corrections job and opted to become a milkman for Cramer Dairies.

My mother, who was working as an executive secretary at a railroad company, met my father a short while after he started working for Cramer Dairies. They fell in love and got married. It was actually the second marriage for my mom, whose first husband had been killed in the war and is buried in Belgium. Together, they had a daughter, Corrine, whom my dad later adopted.

My parents both worked very hard, and by the late 1940s they were able to buy a small home in Chicago. My sister Cynthia was their first child, followed by my brother Clifford, and then me. When I was about two years old, Clifford wound up developing a really bad case of asthma which nearly killed him. The doctors feared the worst, and they told my parents that he needed to live in a warm, dry climate. So, in June of 1953, my parents packed up and moved us all to Tucson, Arizona, in search of a new life and a business to buy.

After two weeks they realized they didn't have enough capital to acquire a business. Struggling financially, they eventually decided to pack up and move yet again, ultimately settling in Twentynine Palms, California, a small town of about 5,000 souls about 45 miles from Palm Springs, in the middle of the Mohave Desert. There, for $1,500, they bought a small home-delivery milk business and renamed it High Desert Food Service. Slowly but surely, they would build their customer base, working extremely long hours for many years. Along the way, our family grew too, with the additions of my three younger siblings Chris, Cathy, and Casey.

In addition to the seven children then living in our small house, my parents took in my dad's folks as well. My grandmother was very sick, and my dad wanted to be able to look after her. My grandparents were good people, and I learned a lot about life from them. The fact that my father insisted upon his parents coming to live with us, versus dumping them in a nursing home, said a lot about him to me and taught me an important lesson.

I learned that it is important to take care of your family, even if you have to make sacrifices to do that. It wasn't like we had a lot of money or anything, because we didn't. My dad just thought taking care of his parents was the right thing to do, so he did it. Besides, he knew that the warmer climate would be good for his mother. That's the way things were done back in the '50s; children took care of their parents in their own homes.

My dad was a really hardworking and resourceful guy. He couldn't afford a mechanic, so he just watched the guys at the local garage whenever they would make repairs, and he wound up teaching himself just about everything he needed to know when it came to keeping his fleet of trucks up and running. He could do everything from changing a tire to replacing an engine. He would work 12 hours during the day making deliveries and then spend four or five hours at night fixing and maintaining the trucks. He knew that if one of the trucks was out of commission, then none of those deliveries could be made. So he did whatever he had to do in order to keep the business going 24/7. The guy never slept; he just worked and worked.

Because there was so much work to be done around the house, loading dock, and shop, my brothers and I were expected to help out doing whatever we could. I learned how to weld, how to take engines apart, and how to build or fix just about anything that I could. I learned a lot from working alongside my dad, but regrettably I am now just like him in the sense that I am too damn cheap and too damn stubborn to hire anyone to fix anything. It is crazy to say, but even if I had $10 million, I would still change the wax seal on my toilet rather than call a plumber. I just couldn't justify paying a guy $200 to do something that I could do. I have a great respect for money. The downside to this is that now I know how to fix things, and I end up with a lot more work to do in my daily life. If my dad had not taught me how to do so many things, I would have more time to put my toes in the sand and a beer in my hand.

My dad just hated to see us kids sitting around. He would constantly find stuff for us to do, or he put my grandfather, known as "the Field Marshal," in charge of keeping us busy. If we were bored, he would make us pick up trash that got caught on the fence. My grandfather used to carry around a piece of wooden lattice with him, and whenever we were goofing off instead of working, he would come up and whack us on the ass with it to straighten us out. If my dad came home and found something that we broke or discovered a job that we were supposed to do but hadn't done yet, he would come in and wake us up in the middle of the night to give us an ass-whipping. Then he would make us go finish the job! To get out of the whipping, we would start to scream as loud as we could, so that Mom could hear us and come running in to save us. "Stop, John! You're going to kill them!" she would yell. My dad would say, "Clara, I haven't touched them yet!" The screaming strategy worked out pretty well for us usually, but if we were going to get a beating, it was actually safer to have Dad beat us; once Mom got ticked off enough to come after one of us, she would grab whatever was in her reach and just start swinging. It could be a flyswatter or a yardstick, it didn't matter. Once she got mad, we would just take off. Luckily I knew that I could run faster scared than she could angry.

I remember once when I was 12 years old, I was helping my dad while he was fixing a truck. He was underneath the truck doing some repairs, and he had me sit next to him and hand him tools as he needed them. (That was his idea of male bonding.) Well, my two brothers were out playing basketball on our new homemade court, which we had made out of a compacted dirt floor and a four-by-four wooden post that held the wooden backboard and basket we had erected. I wanted to play too, so I left my dad's side for a few minutes to go out and take a few shots with my brothers. I figured I would run over and get him what he needed when he called for me.

Well, apparently my father did not appreciate this very much because the next thing I knew he was out there with an axe, chopping down our new basket! He was upset that I would leave him under a truck working while I was out having fun. He said maybe he would like to finish the job so he could shoot some baskets, too. I explained to him that I figured I could work on my speed and quickness when he called for a tool. He didn't buy it. (We did replace the basketball pole.)

As hard-assed as he was, my dad had a compassionate side, too. I remember one time one of our delivery men lost his daughter due to an illness of some sort. My dad felt terrible and decided to give the man some money so that his family could have a proper funeral. Again, we didn't have much money of our own, but my dad felt that it was important, so he gave it to him. I never forgot that. My dad's employees were very loyal to him because he took good care of them and treated them like family. He worked them pretty damn hard, but never harder than he worked. He was honest and fair, and you always knew where you stood with him.

Although my dad worked hard during the week, he tried to be with his family on the weekends as much as possible. He was with the Knights of Columbus, the Catholic benevolent organization, and every Friday he would help cook the halibut for the fish fry. My brothers and sisters and I always looked forward to that. Then, on Sunday mornings after church, he would stop at the Dixie Cream Donut Shop and get a couple dozen donuts, which was a big treat for us. I was even an altar boy and learned how to do the mass in Latin. Going to church was important to my parents; not going wasn't even an option.

Even though we didn't have a lot of money, my dad would make sure that we were able to do little things like that. That was really important to him. He was very principled when it came to money, even to a fault. In fact, I later found out that he never touched any of the money that my mother got from her first husband's Social Security account. Not a dime. As a result, Corrine was able to use that money to go to a private high school and then on to UCLA. My siblings and I never questioned this, because when you're a kid and your family owns a food-service business, you have all the food and ice cream you can eat, so life was pretty good. My dad felt that it was Corrine's money and that she should be able to use it accordingly. Of course, my dad did express to me later that Corrine had developed an elitist attitude and that, if he had to do it over, he would have looked for a better direction in her upbringing. He was always concerned that we know "you are who you are," that "you make of life what you choose to make of it," and that we should never forget what sacrifices our family had to endure to get us where we wanted to be.

According to my mother, I was a pretty mischievous kid. I got into a lot of trouble as a youngster, constantly fighting and arguing with my brothers and sisters. I was feisty, no doubt about it. I even got into it one time with our family dog, Princess. I was about four years old, and she apparently bit my leg. So I chased her down and bit her back, right on the snout. Tit for tat. She never growled at me again after that. I guess I was learning about the power of intimidation from a very early age.

I went to a Catholic grade school called Blessed Sacrament. It was so small that each nun had to teach two grades at the same time. I will never forget my first day of school when I was entering the first grade. I remember standing up with all of the students outside all the classrooms for the Pledge of Allegiance. As soon as it was over, all of the kids took off, including my brother and sister, Clifford and Cynthia. I was just left standing there all by myself, not knowing what to do or where to go.

One of the nuns came over and asked me what grade I was in. I tried to say "first," but because I had a terrible speech impediment, it sounded like I said "fifth." So, she unknowingly put me with the fifth and sixth graders. I was terrified. I mean, I could hardly see over my desk! Luckily, my sister was in the class and was able to steer me back to where I belonged. When I got to my first-grade class, I was pretty upset. Not only was I embarrassed, I was also scared to death of my teacher. She was old and mean and had long whiskers that stuck out of her chin, and she would pluck them out during class! She reminded me of the Wicked Witch from *The Wizard of Oz*.

The nuns wore those old-style habits and were fond of whacking us on our palms with a ruler if we ever got out of line. Needless to say, I would often come home with sore palms. I remember one time getting in trouble during recess. Our basketball bounced over a wall that bordered the convent. There was a strict rule about climbing over that wall, but I figured I was fast enough to get over it and back before anybody knew I was gone. I climbed up over it and landed right square in the middle of where the nuns were having lunch. Knowing that I was totally busted, I just stuck out my palms and decided to take my medicine like a man. Looking back, I guess it would be safe to say that my habit of challenging authority started around this time, too.

Growing up I didn't have a lot of friends. We lived a few miles outside of town in a rural area and didn't have any immediate neighbors. We were pretty isolated out there. There was the Twentynine Palms U.S. Marine Corps base just a few miles away, and we could hear the tanks shooting artillery shells at all hours of the day. After a while, explosions were no big deal, sort of like someone who lives in the city and hears horns and car alarms all day, I suppose. It was lonely, but my parents kept us pretty busy doing chores. We had about 10 acres of land and there was never a shortage of work to be done, that was for sure. Our house was right next to our delivery business, so there were big delivery trucks constantly coming and going, up and down the dirt road in front of our house. We had a big refrigeration building that warehoused all of the milk and dairy products, as well as an eight-stall garage for all of the delivery trucks.

Mealtime around our house was always an adventure. For breakfast we would have a bunch of truck drivers in the house with us because my mom wanted to be sure they went to work on a full stomach. Lunch was chaotic with kids coming and going, but dinner was totally different. Dinner was a big deal. Even though we were all really busy with school activities and work, we always had dinner together. *Always.* That was really important to my mom and dad, so it was a priority in our family. I tried to carry that forward in my own life too, because I think that a lot of problems in the world could be solved by more families just sitting down to break bread and talk. Unfortunately, the world got a little faster, and I regret that I allowed that family custom to eventually drop by the wayside with my own family.

As kids, we all had a lot of chores to do. We all used to fight with each other and complain about all the work we had to do. My least favorite chore by far was cleaning the bathrooms. God, I hated that. We had two bathrooms for 11 people, so as you can imagine they got pretty filthy. But when I finished cleaning it, you could eat off that toilet seat—not that you would want to, but if you were so inclined, you could have! Another one of my chores was shoe polishing. Every Saturday night I had to polish all of the shoes for church the next morning. I could really spit-shine those things so they looked brand new, a little trick I learned from the

Marines that worked part-time for the family business. I was proud of that kind of stuff. I always felt that if you were going to do a job, do it right. I was accused by my friends that the reason I did such a good job and made the shoes so shiny was because it gave me better odds to see up somebody's skirt. Hey, boys will be boys!

We didn't watch much TV or anything like that when I was growing up. In fact, I can remember when we got our first TV; I was about eight years old. But I don't remember sitting around like you see in one of those Norman Rockwell pictures. We only got one channel and it was snowy at best. I remember when we all sat down to watch *Bonanza* for the first time. My mother said, "Wouldn't that be beautiful in color?" So my dad bought one of those plastic covers that went over the screen, with blue on top, tan in the middle, and green on the bottom, and that was our first color TV. What a guy my dad was! Always trying to please my mom.

The truth of the matter was that we were all too busy to watch TV. My parents knew that they had 11 mouths to feed and so they were consumed with their work. They both made deliveries during the day and then at night, when my dad was out fixing trucks, my mom would do the books. Years later I found out that while we were all at school and my mom was at home, my dad was quite fond of coming home for a quick "lunch," if you know what I mean. Way to go, Dad!

Anyway, even though Dad had played some high school football, my brothers and sisters and I really weren't all that interested in sports as kids. We just were not exposed to sports, probably because Blessed Sacrament focused more on academics, as they could not afford an athletic program; after all, with only eight kids in my eighth-grade class, it was a very small school. But our lack of interest in sports soon changed when the Cobbs moved in next door.

The Cobb family owned a body shop, and they had two sports-crazy kids, Jerry and Tom. They were great guys and we hit it off right away. They even showed me my first nudie magazine, which I thought was pretty cool. It was odd having neighbors because prior to that we could run around all day in our underwear—literally. Nobody was around. In fact, when we had to take a piss, we would just whip it out and go, wherever we were. It was that isolated out there.

Anyway, the Cobb brothers went to the public school where they did have athletic programs, and they were big sports fans, so they were the ones who got us into playing and following sports. Whenever we had any free time we would play baseball and basketball, and we even built a high-jumping pit. I eventually convinced my dad to let me play Little League baseball and he even coached our team one year, which was pretty miraculous considering how busy he was with the family business. And, if that wasn't enough, he even took us to a Los Angeles Dodgers game. That was as far from home as I had ever been, and it was really a treat. I am sure he got some free tickets, because he would never spend money on anything like that, but it was fun to be able to see the big boys up close and personal.

Really though, most of our days were spent going to school and then coming home to work. We would spend our days cleaning the yard, washing trucks, loading and unloading trucks, changing tires, and checking the oil and water on the trucks. When that was done we would help put together the orders for each driver for his route the next day. There was a constant flow of trucks going in and out, so it seemingly never ended. Then when the driver would come back in we would have to do a quick inventory on his truck in order to keep track of what was sold. This would continue on the weekends, too. There was just always something to do.

When it came time to go to high school, it was a pretty big adjustment for me. Whereas my eighth-grade Catholic school class had a total of eight kids, my new freshman class totaled more than 250. Because things were so spread out, our high school was comprised of students from five different local communities within a 50-mile radius. I didn't know anybody and really felt like an outsider. And even though I had taken private lessons to correct my speech impediment, I was still pretty shy.

To compensate for that, I immersed myself in sports. That to me was going to be my ticket to acceptance and recognition. I didn't know if I was going to be very good or not, but I knew that I was pretty strong from working so damn hard at home. I went out for the football team that fall and played linebacker on the junior varsity. I would say that I held my own. In fact, I did so well that they moved me up to varsity that October. Not bad for a kid who had never seen a game before. I thoroughly enjoyed hitting people, and I couldn't believe there was actually a sport that allowed me to take out my aggression on people. What a beautiful country.

I also played basketball that winter and ran track in the spring. I was making some friends and was fitting in. I was doing really well athletically as well as academically. I didn't want people to think that I was just a dumb jock, so I worked hard and got pretty good grades. I wanted to prove to people that there was more to me than just sports. Beyond that, I just hated to lose. I didn't want to get beat in *anything*, including academics, so I worked my ass off. Sports had become this amazing outlet for me. Not only was it fun to compete, but it also got me out of working for my dad at home, which was a huge added bonus...or so I thought. He eventually caught on to me and would have the trucks waiting for me when I got home from practice. Bastard!

As a sophomore I made the varsity in football, basketball, and track. I was pretty good in basketball, but I usually fouled out before the game was over. In track, I ran hurdles, pole vaulted, and high jumped. I even found time for a girlfriend. Her name was Beverly, a broad-chested knockout that I was crazy about. When I turned 16, I fixed up a big old 1958 Nash, which I was able to drive to school as well as to see my girl. The seats folded all the way down too, which was like having a built-in bed. God, I loved that car. I also got my own delivery route working for my dad around that same time. It was a lot of hard work, but I enjoyed getting out of the shop. Plus, it was nice to finally be making a few bucks.

Being a delivery man was pretty cool. People were a lot more trusting back in those days, that was for sure.

You see, we couldn't just leave a quart of milk on someone's doorstep out in the desert, so they would give us the keys to their houses in order for us to go in and put it in the refrigerator. Sometimes people would leave us a note telling us what they wanted to order, and other times we would just go in and look in the fridge to figure out what they needed. If they needed eggs or butter or bacon or milk, we would just leave it for them. I could really rearrange a fridge too, let me tell you. We didn't make any money unless we left a lot of food behind, so I made sure to pack and stack as much as humanly possible in there.

Many of our clients were families who worked on the nearby military base or were members of the U.S. Marine Corps. I remember making one delivery where I came across a "B-A-M," or broad-assed Marine. I came into her house and she was sitting there, wearing next to nothing. She looked straight at me, smiled, and said, "There are probably two miles of dick on this base and I can't get eight inches!" I dropped off her milk as fast as I could and made a beeline for the door. She was no Mrs. Robinson, to say the least.

I was too dumb to realize it, but looking back I remember a whole bunch of military wives coming to the door wearing negligees and inviting me in for coffee and donuts. I just figured that they wanted to visit and thought it was sweet that they were comfortable wearing their pajamas around me. Little did I know that I could have been getting some serious action, but I had no idea what was going on. None. In retrospect, I can only kick myself. Oh well. I suppose it must be the Polish in me!

We did some work with the military too, delivering big blocks of ice to the troops out in the desert as they were training. We also made deliveries to the commissaries, which could have been a huge business for my dad had he really pursued it. He probably could have gotten millions of dollars of government business from that base, but he just wasn't savvy enough to figure out how to bid on it. Instead, food companies came all the way up from Los Angeles, which for sure cost the Marines way more money. But that's our government for you, hard at work trying to find the best deals for its citizens.

As a junior I was starting both ways as a linebacker on defense and a running back on offense. I was a pretty strong kid. I never lifted weights or anything like that, but the physical labor of me hauling all of those milk crates around really helped me build up a lot of muscle. I didn't jog either, but I was always moving and on the go, which kept me in good shape. I had an intense desire to prove to the other kids that even though I was from the other side of the tracks, I was just as good if not better than they were. That drove me. My biggest motivation was my fear of failure. I was completely consumed by that fear. I didn't think about anything else.

As busy as I was with school and sports, I still found time to work. In fact, I was even put to work during school hours under a program called "work experience," where I would deliver truckloads of small milk containers to all the local schools during the first period of the day. I would get up at 5:30 every morning and load my truck like clockwork. I worked on Saturdays too, doing home-delivery routes in order to give our drivers a day off. Even if I had a track meet on Saturday, I would compete and then change back into my white milkman's uniform to go back to work. Sometimes I would even make a few bucks by selling a few dozen frozen popsicles at the meet. My mom paid me $20 per week as a salary, but I was always interested in making an extra buck wherever I could.

On Sundays we had to work on the trucks, doing repairs and maintenance in order to keep them running. As a result, I didn't get to socialize a lot on the weekends. I had a few buddies and we would drink beers together, but I never really partied in high school or anything like that. Whatever free time I did have, I wanted to spend it with Beverly. Having a girlfriend really cut into my work time though, and that really pissed off my dad. She lived about 25 miles away in Yucca Valley, so whenever I went to go see her my dad made sure to always have something for me to do along the way. It seemed like every time I went to go pick her up for a date I would have to drop something off at one of our commercial customers in the area or change a tire on a truck at our Yucca Valley location. Hell, he might have 10 deliveries lined up for me along the way. That was his way of punishing me, I think. Anyway, the earliest I ever got to Beverly's house for a date was 30 to 45 minutes late. It really didn't bother me all that much, but Beverly had a difficult time understanding the situation. I just told her she would have to get over it. That may have been the reason we never attended many high school parties.

My senior year was a lot of fun. Football was going well and I had become one of the stars of our team. As a running back I had several games where I scored multiple touchdowns and really dominated. I was winning awards and accolades from local newspapers. I was known for being tough too, which I thought was pretty cool. I wouldn't back down from anybody and had earned a reputation. I wasn't a dirty player, but I was certainly very confident. Maybe even arrogant.

My parents never missed a game, and that meant a lot to me. Some of our road games were several hours away, which meant that my dad would have to come home and then work all night. But it was nice to know that it meant enough to him to do that for me. I knew he was proud of me, but he would never say anything like that to me. Never. That was okay though. I didn't need that. In retrospect, I think that my playing football did more for him than him being there did for me.

After the season I was invited to play in an all-star game in nearby Riverside. I had earned all-league honors for three straight years, but this was a big deal because it was for all of the top kids from Southern California. Despite the fact that I tore up my knee in the last game of the year, I went and I held my own against the kids from the bigger schools. Playing football in college had never even entered my mind prior to that, but afterward it looked like a real possibility.

Even though I was in the local papers, I didn't get any major media coverage or anything like that playing in Twentynine Palms. Luckily I had a couple of coaches—Dick Trone and Al Peyton—who really took an interest in me. They put together some film footage and wrote hundreds of letters on my behalf which they then sent out to colleges. As a result, I wound up getting scholarship offers from about two dozen schools, including Utah, Utah State, Arizona, Arizona State, San Diego State, Cal-Berkeley, and Wyoming. Dick Trone and Al Peyton were the reason I got to play college football; without them I never would have played. I am convinced of that.

The school I was most intrigued with was the University of Wyoming, which had just played in the Sugar Bowl. They played in the Western Athletic Conference and were one of the better schools in the area at the time. Plus, Coach Peyton had gone there and he thought that they would be a good fit for me. They offered me a full ride without even visiting, but I really wanted to go check the place out. I didn't have enough money to fly up there, so my dad offered to buy me a ticket. I was totally blown away. It was $129, which was a lot of money for him, but I gladly accepted it. When I got up there the coaches told me that if I signed a letter of intent, they would reimburse me for my ticket. Feeling guilty about my dad's $129 investment, I wound up signing it.

I remember asking my dad for his advice on where he thought I should go before I left for Wyoming. He just smiled and said, "This is your choice and yours alone." He told me that if I went where he thought I should go, then it would be too easy for me to quit. He wanted it to be my decision. He said, "You're 17 years old. You think you know it all. You are going away to college and are becoming a man. It is about time you make your own decisions." He reiterated that no matter how tough it got, and no matter how much I wanted to quit and come back home, it was my decision and mine alone. He wanted me to fully understand that I was making my own bed and that I was going to have to sleep in it. Sure enough, there would be many, many times in college when I wanted to walk away and quit. But because of what my old man had told me, I couldn't. God, that pissed me off. I never wanted him to be able to say, "I told you so." No way. Failing was not an option for me. I was not going to disappoint him with the first big decision I ever made in my life. What is really funny is that it was the first time I ever asked my father for advice, and the best advice he gave me was no advice, other than to make my own decision!

Looking back, I am so thankful for that scholarship because I didn't really have a backup plan. I probably would've married Beverly and worked for my dad. Who knows? Going to Vietnam was always a possibility, too. My age group was the first to be put into the lottery. For better or for worse, my draft number was like No. 359, so I never got the opportunity to go. Looking back, I regret that. My dad fought in World War II, and I would have liked to have represented my country in that way. Interestingly, my brother told me just a few years ago about a conversation he had with my dad one time about it. Dad apparently said that if any of his three sons had gotten drafted, he would have found a way to get them to Canada. I couldn't believe it. My dad was a pretty patriotic guy, so to hear that was pretty shocking to me. Anyway, even to this day I still try to give back by going to the VA hospitals to sign autographs and do whatever I can to cheer those people up. They are heroes in my opinion. No doubt about it.

I graduated from high school in May of 1968 and worked my ass off that summer, eager to earn as much money as I could before heading off to college. I remember wanting to spend a lot of time with Beverly over those few months too, because we were both going to different schools that fall. As usual, whenever I went up to see her, my dad would load up a bunch of deliveries for me. Now, I understood and accepted my responsibilities for my family business, but one time I got really upset about having to do all of that extra stuff and I just snapped.

It was the Fourth of July weekend, and I had put in a full day of work and was anxious to go see my girlfriend. Just as I was about to leave, my dad starts loading boxes into my car. "Take this stuff up to Yucca," he said very matter-of-factly. "No," I snapped, "I don't want to take it up there. I don't want to be late." "Yes, you will!" he screamed. "No, I won't!" I yelled back. With that, he came charging at me! Instinctively, I shoved him and knocked him over some milk crates. He landed flat on his back and I just took off.

I could hear him chasing me, so I ran straight to my room. I slammed the door and started packing my suitcase. "Where the hell do you think you are going?" he screamed. "I am leaving. I'll just go to college early," I said. "You're asking me to make these deliveries, and then pick Beverly up, and drive back to the Marine base for the fireworks display, when you know damn well I won't have enough time to do both. It's not fair! You're abusing me, and not allowing me to have a life of my own, and I am sick of it." (Boy, have I heard "It's not fair!" a number of times from my six children since then!)

My dad looked at me, and realizing that I meant business, he said, "You can't leave." "Why not?" I asked. "Because your mother will kill us both!" he said. He was right! So I stopped, grabbed my keys, and headed for Beverly's, without the boxes. My dad and I never spoke about it again.

I think my dad realized that I was a man that day. His little boy had grown up, and I think that was hard for him to accept. He couldn't control me anymore. I had earned his respect. But to this day I lost a little bit of respect for myself. To shove my dad and rob him of his pride was not one of my better moments, and I still regret it to this day. Even though I finally pushed back and stood up for myself, I still wish I had never done it.

I worked hard for the rest of the summer and then packed up for good that fall when it came time to head off to college. My grandfather wound up driving with me up to Laramie, Wyoming, which was about a 1,000-mile trip. We drove my '65 Comet, even though I wasn't sure if it was going to make it or not. It was pretty neat getting to spend that quality time with my grandfather. Even though I grew up with the guy, I never really got to know him as much as I would have liked.

For years he and my grandmother lived in an Airstream trailer on our property until my dad was able to build them a one-room house right next to ours. It was really hard on my grandfather when my grandmother passed away. He didn't talk about it very much, but I could just tell. My grandpa was tough, just like my dad was. He used to put us kids to work whenever my mom and dad were gone making deliveries. My brothers and I would get all excited when they were gone, figuring we could goof off all day and play basketball. Once my grandpa got wind of that, however, those plans would come to a screeching halt. He would put us to work doing whatever he could think of, whether it was mowing the lawn, raking the dirt, or just picking weeds. He had a strong work ethic, too. He used to have a limousine business back in Chicago, but some mobsters felt like he was hurting their business, so they put stink bombs in his fleet of limos one night which essentially ruined them. After that he became a trolley operator.

I think it was hard for him to leave Chicago to come live with us, but he made the best of it and I learned a lot about life from him. I remember one time when I was home from college, I got a bottle of Jack Daniels and went to see him. I said, "Grandpa, tell me about your life story." He just looked at me like I was crazy and said, "Listen you damn fool, why the hell didn't you ask me that question 10 years ago when I could still remember?" My grandpa was a pretty funny guy.

2

COLLEGE MAN

"I wasn't a pro football fan,
to be honest.
My main motivation
for playing football in college
was to get a scholarship.
I never dreamed of playing in the NFL
like a lot of other kids did.
That just wasn't me."

When I got to campus, my grandpa helped me move into my dormitory, Hill Hall, before catching a flight home. I was so excited to take it all in. I remember the oddest things about that day, including the fact that it was the first basement I had ever seen. We didn't have basements in California because of earthquakes, so that was unique. My roommate was a guy by the name of Jim Eastlack, an offensive lineman from New Jersey who would go on to become a very successful executive with British Petroleum. He was a great guy, and I enjoyed living with him. We spent many an evening in deep conversation about the meaning of life. Sure we did! When Jim first told me that his dad was in oil, I thought he was rich. But then he told me that his dad delivered heating oil to homeowners.

Football practice started right away and I was anxious to prove myself. The freshman coach was a guy by the name of Jack Taylor. He was a great guy and we would become good friends later in life. The level of competition was obviously a lot tougher than where I came from, which was somewhat intimidating to me. I was also a little taken aback when I noticed that there were around 115 freshmen football players there on full rides. I realized I wasn't all that special, and there would be a lot of work involved in making the football team as a starter.

When I came into training camp, they listed me as a tight end. I assumed that I would be given an opportunity to compete for a starting job. I wasn't trying to be a cocky freshman or anything, I just figured that I was good enough to play and wanted to show what I could do. Our starting quarterback was a kid by the name of Gary Fox and our starting tight end just so happened to be his best friend from high school back in Montana. Well, I could immediately see the writing on the wall. Even though I was bigger, faster, and stronger than this kid was, I knew that there was no way in hell I was going to be playing tight end with him around.

I thought about trying to play running back because I had been pretty damn good in high school, but I knew that the two guys ahead of me on the depth chart—Frosty Franklin at halfback and Jeff Howe at fullback—weren't going anywhere. Frosty was a tough kid from Powell, Wyoming, and Jeff, you guessed it, was a running back from the same high school as the quarterback and the tight end. It was my first life lesson in politics winning out over talent, but I wasn't about to buck the system.

In my mind, I knew who I was, and I knew that I was better than them and that I could outrun both of them. I ran the 40-yard dash in around 4.6 seconds, whereas both of them were around 4.9. It wasn't even close. I was bigger and tougher, too. Coming from a small town hurt me though; I could see that right away. They just assumed that you didn't play against any good competition and you were judged accordingly. It sucked, but that was just the way it was.

Eventually, I just told the coaches that I was willing to play anywhere that they wanted me to. So they moved me to offensive tackle, a position I had never played before. Hell, I didn't care; I just wanted to play. Playing on the offensive line was a big adjustment for me. I was 6'3" and 235 pounds, certainly not huge by today's standards, but big enough in those days. Plus, I was pretty quick. There was a pretty big learning curve ahead of me, so I tried to stay humble and just fit in with the other guys.

The coaches were really tough on us. Seventeen freshmen quit after the first day, and another 40 would join them before the end of the season. The coaches wanted to weed out the weakest kids, and that is exactly what happened. I didn't want to lose my scholarship, so I worked my ass off. We had a pretty damn good freshman team. We didn't just beat teams, we *destroyed* them. We beat Colorado twice, as well as Colorado State and Air Force, and ultimately went undefeated.

We were a rowdy bunch too, that was for sure. We celebrated early and often. We had some strong personalities on the team and we weren't afraid to let our hair down. We got in a lot of trouble, from starting trash cans on fire in the dorms, to starting food fights in the cafeteria, to having women in our rooms, to getting into brawls at campus bars, to crashing frat parties. We didn't take any shit from anybody either, including the guys on the varsity. By the end of the season, we had become pretty cocky, no doubt about it.

Most of the kids who were on the team had come from larger schools, and a lot of them came from wealthy families. Hell, the Wyoming campus was bigger than my entire hometown. So again I had to find a way to be accepted. I ended up getting into a few fights with some of my teammates. It was like high school all over again in some regards, and I felt like an outsider. I always looked for acceptance but understood that I had to earn it. The kids from the city were pretty cruel with the put-downs they would throw at each other. I had never been exposed to that growing up. In our family the "N" word was simply not tolerated. I remember saying it once, and my dad knocked me upside my head so hard that I fell out of my chair. Lesson learned.

It was real cutthroat out there, with a lot of competition for playing time. Practices were rough. Whenever we screwed up we were punished by running until we nearly dropped. But I worked hard and never let the coaches think that I could be broken. All of that hard work that I endured as a kid working for my dad was paying off. While a lot of the other kids were getting tired and quitting, I was only getting stronger. It didn't take me very long to figure out how to adapt and use my strengths to my advantage.

I got my first taste of what it was like to play dirty during practice one day when the coaches asked a handful of freshmen to run some plays against the varsity. I asked one of the assistants, Burt Gustafson, how he wanted me to play: no contact, half speed, or full speed. I didn't know. He screamed, "Dammit, I want you to block the guy like it's a goddamn game! Just run the goddamn play like it's drawn up!" So I went out there and lined up against the team's star defensive tackle, Larry Nels. It was a pass play, and as soon as he came at me, I hit him high and then dropped down and cut his legs out from underneath him. He went down like a ton of bricks and started writhing in pain. In football practice, to cut a guy or to chop him at the knees is a serious no-no. It can be a career-ender, so it is very frowned upon.

Well, as soon as this happened, the defensive coordinator, Fritz Shurmur, came charging at me. I was down on the ground, so he started kicking me in the ribs and in the helmet. He then grabbed me and started to read me the riot act. "You fucking asshole! You punk! What are you fucking doing, cutting our star player?" Needless to say, I was pretty intimidated at that moment. He had my attention, that was for sure. Shurmur was a real pain in the ass. He was a mean drill-sergeant type and tried to intimidate through fear. He also had the defense that led the nation in 1967, so he was very protective of his defensive players, especially his star players.

From that point on the guys on the varsity called me a "Jap," meaning I was the enemy—a WWII reference for pulling a sneak attack, I suppose. I was a marked man after that, which really sucked. I was ostracized right then and there, which made things a lot tougher for me. I dealt with it on my own terms, though. If a guy thought that I was an asshole, then I would go on the offensive and take the fight to him before he could take it to me. Either way, I think that was a defining moment for me as a football player, because it was at that point that I started to get a reputation for being a badass. With that title, however, came a certain level of respect. I also learned that fear and intimidation can be powerful tools to have in your arsenal.

In spring practice the coaches had me try out at both offensive and defensive tackle. They wanted to evaluate me, which meant I had to spend a half hour each day working under both the offensive and defensive coordinators. I loved playing defense and was really good at it, but since Shurmur was the defensive coach, I chose to play offense just so I didn't have to deal with that asshole. My favorite coach was a guy by the name of Tom Tatum. He was a graduate assistant with the freshman team who also worked on the side as a rodeo clown. He was a real tough sonofabitch, just crazy. I loved him. We immediately hit it off, and I wound up learning a great deal from him. He was full of all sorts of tricks that he had learned from dodging bulls. He was the one who taught me how to leg whip guys, using your whole body as a weapon to get them on the ground where you could really take advantage of them. "Leg whip" is a phrase I was accused of coining years later in the NFL, and I sort of become synonymous with that devastating move. But I didn't invent it. In reality, it was around for a long time before I came along and used it with much more proficiency.

I survived that first season and wound up doing well in school. Everything about being there was an adjustment though, especially going from the blistering-hot desert to the freezing cold. That was tough. Plus, to go from the loose lifestyle of Californians to the conservative culture of Wyoming was like night and day. Talk about polar-opposite places. Once the season was over, I had a little more time to myself and I was anxious to spend more time with Beverly. She and I tried to do the long-distance thing that first year. She was going to school near her folks back home and had an apartment. I was in love with her and even sent her $15 per month of my laundry allowance money in order to help her out.

Everything fell apart, however, when I decided to surprise her one time by driving down to see her. When I got there, I found a note she had written to one of her girlfriends which said that she was just using me for the money I was sending her. (Back then, $15 was a lot of money.) In reality, she was screwing another guy on the side. When she got home from wherever she was, I showed her the letter and called her out on it. I was pissed. She just looked at me, horrified, and then started bitching at me about sneaking around her apartment and reading her private letters. So I just left, and that was the end of Beverly. I was pretty broken up over it. I think that made me really distrust women. Even to this day, I still struggle with opening up to members of the opposite sex. I have a difficult time giving fully of myself and letting them into my soul.

That summer I worked at an open-pit salt mine out in this tiny town in California, Amboy, as a dynamiter. Literally the only thing in this town was a truck stop, because it was the exact halfway point between Los Angeles and Las Vegas. I lived at home, and a bunch of my buddies and I would get up at 5:00 in the morning and drive out there together, about an hour away. It was a crazy job. I would sit out in this shed all day, sometimes by myself, wiring fuses together with the blasting caps. The glue that we used to hold it together was really toxic, but I didn't know that at the time. As a result, I would come out after being in there for hours and hours and could barely walk. I didn't know what the hell was going on, but the Mexican workers would all just laugh at me. They knew that stuff was bad news.

When I wasn't doing that, I was working another job collecting chlorine and building railroad tracks for the hoppers to haul the rock salt back to the mill. It was hot, dirty work. At the end of the day my buddies and I would stop at this little bar on the way home and get pitchers of beer. We were all just dead and ready to collapse by the time we got there. Then, on the weekends, I would work around the house, helping out my dad any way that I could. I was busier than hell. At the end of the summer I had almost saved enough to buy a Mustang but was about a thousand bucks short. My old man wanted me to have it though, so he helped me out. It was totally unexpected, but I gladly accepted it.

It meant a lot to me that he would do that and I really appreciated it. I had always had a love affair with Mustangs and couldn't wait to drive it around campus that fall.

My sophomore season would prove to be an interesting one, to say the least. When I got back to school we were all saddened by the death of one of our teammates, quarterback Ed Synakowski, who had drowned in a boating accident. Ironically, I was out driving around with my roommate at the time when we heard about it on the radio. We just happened to be right near the lake where it happened, so we drove over and actually saw the rescue workers removing his body from the water. We were all pretty shook up over it. He was a senior and a really good guy, and it was a real tragedy.

Back on the field, I wound up starting at right tackle that season and was anxious to prove myself amongst the big boys. We started out that season on fire! In our first four games, we beat Arizona, Air Force, Colorado State, and UTEP to start the season at 4–0. Everything changed, however, in Week 5 when we hosted Brigham Young University. What transpired during that game would infamously become known as the "Black 14" incident. Prior to the BYU game, all of the African American players on our team got together and decided to wear black armbands in protest of the Church of Jesus Christ of Latter-day Saints' policy not to permit African Americans to become priests.

The 14 players were repeatedly warned by the coaches and university staff ahead of time not to wear the armbands, but they decided to do so anyway. Our coach, Lloyd Eaton, was opposed to mixing football and politics, especially at a state-run university. So he decided to kick them all off the team, including about a half dozen starters. It was a huge deal, and it was all over the national news.

We went ahead and played the BYU game anyway, and we crushed them 40–7. But it was really ugly off the field. There were fans waving confederate flags and we even had to have extra security. You know, I respected the players' decision to protest, but they really screwed the rest of us with the way they did it. We never really recovered from the whole thing, and in the end I think it was a pretty selfish thing to do.

As a team, you can't just do something and think it won't affect everybody else. Afterward, several of the black players even picketed our practices, calling the white players "honkies," "whiteys," "racists," and a few other choice words. I understood that they were upset, but there was nothing I could do about it. Hell, I would have worn an armband to support them if they had asked, but it was the coach who made the decision to expel them, not me. Years later, I found out that a lot of the players had been convinced to do what they did by some prominent black activist organizations. Some of the players even got death threats warning them not to back out. I was pretty shocked when I heard that.

The wheels fell off our team after that, and we wound up losing our last four games. We were so shorthanded that we actually suited up our equipment manager. If that wasn't bad enough, we even enlisted one of our male cheerleaders to be our long snapper. It was the craziest damn thing. Jim Eastlack had hurt his shoulder and he couldn't play, so the coaches had him work with this cheerleader to toughen the guy up a little bit. This kid would snap the ball and Jimmy would immediately knock him to the ground, ass over tea kettle. The kid would then get up, brush himself off, and do it all over again. They wanted to simulate what it was going to be like during a game, and in their eyes that was the best way to do it. I felt really sorry for that poor sonofabitch. I remember looking over at Jimmy one time during practice and just laughing. There he was, with his arm in a sling, whacking this poor kid over and over again, just tormenting him. He looked over at me and said, "Conrad, this is the goddamnedest job I have ever had in my life!"

Sadly, I broke my wrist during our last game, a 41–14 beating by the University of Houston. Then, to make matters worse, I had to have knee surgery that off-season. It would be the second of many, many surgeries for me. Then, just when I thought things couldn't get much worse, an incident occurred just before I was going to drive home for the summer that really pissed me off. You see, shortly after school got out we had a big steak fry for the team. I was standing in line waiting to get my food when Coach Eaton walked by. He looked at me and saw that I had started to grow some long sideburns, which were pretty trendy in those days. Well, he was old-school and prohibited anyone on the team from having them, thinking people who did were dope-smoking hippies or something. He had a rule about them, which I knew about, but I figured that since school was out I was free to do whatever I wanted. Anyway, he walked over to me and grabbed the empty plate out of my hand. He then proceeded to whack it over my head. "Go back to the dorm and shave your goddamn sideburns," he yelled. "Then come see me when they are gone."

So I went and shaved them off and met him in his office after the barbeque. "You know the rules, Conrad," he said. "That'll cost you your book money and your fees for one year." Just like that, he cut the book allowance out of my scholarship, which was really shitty in my opinion. I mean, school was over, and this was on my own time. I think it was pay-back for my chop block the season before, but who knows? Luckily, my offensive line coach, Bill Baker, was in charge of the athletic bookstore and picked the players he wanted to run it. So you can guess who got the job. The funny thing about the books in this store was that most of the books were used but had never been opened. While working in the store, an older player explained to me how I could get that money back. He showed me that by using sandpaper to rub off the official stamp that read "ATHLETICS," I could return the books for money at the student bookstore. It was a little dishonest, and I knew it, but I just figured you gotta do what you gotta do sometimes in order to get by. Besides, when opportunity presents itself, you have to take advantage of the situation.

There was definitely some preferential treatment that went on behind the scenes in those days. Hell, we had some kids on the team who were flat broke, yet they somehow wound up flying home for Christmas. I remember one time one of my buddies on the team, our starting running back, had his motorcycle stolen. He was all bummed out because he still owed $500 on it. So he went to see one of the coaches about it. He apparently told him what happened and the coach simply reached under his desk and pulled out a shoe box. He opened it up and took out $500, which he then handed to my buddy like it was no big deal. When I heard about it, I was shocked. I told my buddy that I didn't know that kind of stuff was going on. He then looked at me, smiled, and said, "All you had to do was ask." Needless to say, I never "asked" for anything, so I never got anything. I never got a dime, other than the book money. I was never given money to take any new recruits out on the town. One of my buddies had two recruits per weekend, and he was making an extra $50 every weekend! I look back on those days and wonder why I was on the outside looking in. I guess I didn't want to make waves, so I just did my own thing. I was living in my own little world, maybe because I supposedly had lived such a sheltered life. Looking back, I am not sure that was the smartest thing for me to do.

I worked that off-season at home for my dad, driving milk trucks. It was good to be home and to see my old friends. When I headed back to school that fall for my junior season, I was looking forward to getting out on the field. Sadly, however, the fallout from the Black 14 incident had spilled over into the next season, and we wound up winning only one game. It was brutal. We lost a lot of recruits, and wherever we went, black protestors would come out in force to let our coaches know how they felt about them. The one silver lining was the fact that our one win came over rival Colorado State, which was only about 50 miles away. We hated those bastards, so beating them was at least a decent consolation prize.

I did learn a few things that season though. There was this defensive tackle, Charlie Wilson, who I would go against all the time in one-on-one pass-rush drills in practice. I used to just beat him up; I mean I absolutely *destroyed* him. It wasn't personal; he was a nice guy and a good friend of mine. And I wasn't being dirty either. For whatever reason, I had gotten inside this poor guy's head and he had convinced himself that no matter how hard he tried, he couldn't beat me. He would sit in his dorm room before practice on days when he knew that we were going to face each other, smoking a cigarette, and he'd say, "I am going to quit today, I am going to quit today..." Charlie would eventually make it out onto the field, late, and he would just dread lining up against me. On pass plays, he couldn't even get out of his stance. I was too quick for him and would knock him over. On rushing plays, I would charge out of my stance and pancake him, knocking him down to the ground.

I couldn't let him beat me, but I didn't want to embarrass the guy either. I practically begged the coaches to let me go against somebody else, but they thought that they could make him a better player by having him go up against me all the time. His confidence was shot. Mentally, he was busted. He was broken. They would scream at him too: "Come on you fat cocksucker, move your damn feet! Let's go, you pussy!" It was sad, it really was. He was totally demoralized. The compassionate side of me felt really bad for the guy. He eventually just had enough and quit. I learned a lot from Charlie though. I learned that you can never give up if you want something bad enough. And I also learned that half of the battle is in your head.

After the season I just did my own thing and tried to stay out of trouble. I actually studied quite a bit. I think I was finding myself, so to speak. I hadn't declared a major but was really interested in political science and child psychology. I enjoyed history and I liked working with computers too, which were something new at the time. I even thought about becoming a lawyer, because I loved to argue and was pretty good at it. I especially liked working with kids though, and even got into doing some volunteer teaching and tutoring at a local boys' home in the area. Becoming a teacher was something I could definitely see myself doing.

I liked going to the library because not only was it a good place to study, it was a good place to pick up hot, smart girls. From there we would go out and get some beers, which was all a part of the thrill of the chase, which I loved. Getting out of the dorm and going to the library was really good for me. I was able to concentrate and get my work done without any distractions. Most of my teammates never figured that out. They wondered why they got bad grades and it was so obvious to me. I think the difference between being an A or B student and a C or D student is only about an hour a night of studying. That's it. You had to put in the time though; there were no shortcuts. I had a strong work ethic, so I worked hard and got good grades. It was important to me.

That summer I worked doing construction at a coal gasification plant during the day and then ran a bar at night in the small town of Diamondville, Wyoming . I was living with a buddy of mine at his mother's house in the nearby town of Kemmerer. Working at the bar was a real trip. I was only 20 years old at the time, and even though the drinking age was 21, nobody ever asked me my age, so I got away with it. We had gambling going on in the back room, and on Friday nights we would have strippers come up from Salt Lake City. To help the strippers make extra money, I would go around the bar and collect $5 from all the construction workers, and the girls would then dance without their panties. I was always doing my part to help other people.

Sometimes things would get out of hand and I would have to step in to keep the peace. I was not a big fighter back then, believe it or not, but I was pretty damn tough. If a drunk patron ever started a fight, I would grab him by his esophagus and cut off the air to his windpipe. I would then calmly ask him if he wanted me to rip his throat out or if he wanted to settle down instead. I always gave him a choice. That usually ended the problem pretty quickly. On the rare occasion that I did fight someone, I made sure it was quick. I was usually a two-hit fighter: I hit the other guy, and he hit the ground. I never really enjoyed that part of the job. In fact, it was better if I could get them to calm down, because I would always receive extra tip money from them.

I think I only got about four hours of sleep a night that summer. The money was great though, so I just sucked it up and worked my ass off. I was clearing like $600 a week, which was fantastic money in those days. I wound up socking it away and later bought my first piece of real estate, a little duplex in Laramie, while I was still in college. I learned a lot about saving money from my mom and dad and I wanted to invest it in something that would give me a good return. This would only be the beginning of my lifelong love/hate relationship with real estate.

It was hard to believe, but in the fall of 1971, I hit the field as a senior. Lloyd Eaton got tired of the bullshit surrounding the Black 14 incident and decided to call it a day. He was really a great coach and a wonderful motivator and always talked about "Wyoming Pride." He reminded us that he had recruited smaller and quicker players, and assured us that we would always beat the other team with our speed. He would tell us, and I remember it to this day, that he never measured a man by the size of his body but by the size of his heart and by his level of commitment. He was a real Paul Harvey–type of talker. I think he could have run for governor of Wyoming and won if it wasn't for the Black 14 incident.

As luck would have it, when Eaton resigned, my old friend, defensive coordinator Fritz Shurmur, took over as our new head coach. *Just great*, I thought. We lose a really great coach because of this political distraction, and he is replaced with none other than my nemesis. I had played offensive tackle for my first three years but decided to make the switch to defensive tackle for my senior year. Shurmur had wanted his best guys on defense and I was happy to oblige. I wasn't good enough to play for Shurmur when he was the defensive coordinator, but once he became head coach, it was a different story. It worked out well for me too, because I wound up earning defensive MVP honors. Needless to say, it was a lot of fun to finally be able to bash people around as the aggressor for a change.

My senior year was a lot of fun, both on and off the field. My roommate that season was Ken Hustad, the tight end from Montana. Our dorm room doubled as a cocktail lounge after the home games. We even had a huge bar in there. It was nuts. We would charge a buck a head, plus a buck per drink, so we made some good cash on the side. We threw some parties that got pretty wild. One of the best things about rooming with Ken was the fact that I met his freshman sister Carla. She was a tall, gorgeous blonde, a real knockout. We started dating and I fell in love with her. Their dad had just passed away though, and Ken didn't want her settling down with me for whatever reason. I was older and wiser and had been around the block, if you know what I mean. Ken wasn't thrilled about having his baby sister dating a guy like me, so he basically broke us up. I would have gladly married her had it not been for that. But it just wasn't meant to be.

As a team we played better than the year before, but certainly not as well as we would have liked. We ultimately finished with a 5–6 record, which included a couple of big wins over Arizona and Colorado State. Perhaps my most memorable game came against rival Colorado, which was the same team we trounced four years earlier as freshmen. The problem was that we had only 11 players left on our roster from that team, whereas they had retained most of their entire squad. They crushed us 56–13. What I remember the most, however, was the fact that it was colder than hell. It had snowed the night before, and for some reason some genius used a fire hose to clean the stadium seats and stairways. It would have worked great had he used salt water, but instead it wound up being a hockey rink in there. Fans were slipping and sliding everywhere.

Incidentally, I got into a fight and got tossed out of the game. Believe it or not, that was the first and only game I was ever thrown out of in high school or college. Afterward, as I was leaving the field, I saw my nemesis Coach Shurmur jogging toward me to chew my ass out. Just as he was about to lay into me, he got nailed right in the face with a snowball from a drunk fan. His headset and hat went flying, and he just stood there stunned. I used the opportunity to slip away into the crowd so he couldn't catch me. He was so pissed about getting drilled that he forgot about me getting ejected. Oh well, it served the bastard right!

After the season was over I remember sitting in the locker room, reflecting on the blur that the last four years had been. I had worked hard both on and off the field and was even rewarded with All-WAC academic honors to boot; I was very proud of that accomplishment. Looking back, that award means more to me today than the Pro Bowl honors I got in the NFL. I just couldn't believe my college career was over. It had been quite a journey. Interestingly, of the 115 freshman football players who came in on full rides, only 11 were left standing at the end. Everybody else either quit or got cut somewhere along the way. We had such a strong freshman team too; it was so sad to think about how those coaches had managed to run off so many of our top players. Had we been able to remain together as a unit, there is no doubt in my mind that we would have played in a few bowl games.

I had a really strong season and was hoping to get nominated by Coach Shurmur to play in one of the annual all-star games for college football's top seniors, such as the Senior Bowl, the Blue-Gray Classic, or the East-West Shrine Game. I would have loved to have played in one more game before hanging up my pads for good. Plus, I figured that the recognition would have been nice, too. For some reason though, Shurmur didn't want to do a damn thing for me. I remember going into his office to talk to him about it and him handing me a bunch of applications, basically saying, "If you want to go, then you fill them out." What a prick! He was certainly not like the coaches I had in high school. One would have thought that having a player go to the postseason bowls would have helped his recruiting that spring. I have always wondered why he didn't do the little things that would've helped him build a winning program. With no endorsement from my coach, I didn't get to play in any of those all-star games, and with that, I figured I was done with football.

I kind of went my own way after college. In fact, after the season was over I wound up moving in with a law professor who was a friend of mine. As a result, I hung out with a lot of his friends, who were local businessmen and professional people from the community. It was an older group, and those were the people who I wanted to socialize with. I have always enjoyed hanging around with older people; even when I played in the NFL, while most guys were hanging around with people in their twenties, I was hanging around with guys in their forties. I just felt more comfortable around them. Maybe it was because when I was growing up I was always around older people, the truck drivers and the adults I met when I was making deliveries or going over their invoices.

From there, I continued my studies and was preparing to graduate that winter and become a teacher. That was my plan. Then, on February 2, 1972, everything changed when I found out that I had been selected in the fifth round of the NFL Draft by the St. Louis Cardinals. I had been out mountain climbing between Cheyenne and Laramie with some buddies at the time and had no idea that the draft was even going on. Honestly, it hadn't even entered my mind. Anyway, when I got back to my dorm room a reporter from the *Laramie Boomerang* newspaper called me and asked me how I felt about being drafted by the Cardinals. I just sort of laughed, thinking it was a joke.

Not really thinking, I said, "The baseball team?" The reporter thought I was being funny, so he laughed, but I really wasn't. I just laughed along, not wanting him to think I was an idiot. But in reality, I didn't have a clue. It hadn't dawned upon me that the Chicago Cardinals football team had moved to St. Louis 12 years earlier. I wasn't a pro football fan, to be honest. My main motivation for playing football in college was to get a scholarship. I never dreamed of playing in the NFL like a lot of other kids did. That just wasn't me. In fact, it's funny to think about now, but back in the dorm my roommate Jim and I were two of the only people to have a TV. But rather than watching football on Sundays like all of our buddies wanted us to, we watched *Star Trek* instead. We would refuse to switch channels and it would really piss everybody off. We just weren't that interested in the game. Funny how life works out when you think you're on the right road and then all of a sudden, someone changes the road.

Anyway, once I found out he was serious, I was like, "Holy shit, I'm going to the show." I made it. It was actually a pretty cool feeling. Interestingly, I later found out that Shurmur had told some of the NFL scouts who were interested in me that I wasn't good enough to make it. When I heard that, it really motivated me to prove that sonofabitch wrong. I have no idea why he would have said something like that. What an asshole. I was the only guy on the team who had been drafted and you would think, again, this would be a feather in the cap for the program. Apparently he didn't see it that way. Hell, I really didn't care what he thought, but I have to admit that his attitude made me push myself just a little bit harder. I figured I would go do "this NFL thing" until I had to go find a "real job." My main focus was to do everything in my power to make the Cardinals' roster that fall. I was on a mission.

Ironically, Shurmur went on to coach defense in the NFL for six different teams, and so I once again had the opportunity to beat up on his defensive players. Payback is a real bitch! I guess it just goes to show that, even though life is not always fair, sometimes things work out if you wait long enough.

3

CUTTING MY TEETH
WITH THE CARDINALS

*"I never really understood
the whole 'playing dirty' thing,
to tell you the truth.
Sure, I played mean and nasty,
and sure I tried to knock guys
on their asses.
But I never deliberately went out
to try to hurt anyone."*

In early 1972, a few weeks after the NFL Draft, the Cardinals flew me down to St. Louis to meet with the team's owner, Bill Bidwell. I remember talking to him a bit about the terms of the contract. I said that since I was now in the NFL, I was sure that the Cardinals would want me to represent the team by being well dressed, and of course that takes money. Bill had told me to look at the way he was dressed, and said it's not that hard to look presentable. I didn't realize it at the time, but afterward, it dawned on me that Bill always looked like an unmade bed! Other than that, I don't remember much about meeting with him, as he wasn't what you would expect an owner of a professional football team would be like. I do remember getting together with the stewardess from my flight later that night...but I digress. Anyway, I met some of the coaches and they put me through a few drills. I came in at 230 pounds and ran a 40-yard dash in 4.6, which totally blew them away. From there, I went back to Wyoming to finish up my last semester of school.

I got busy that spring preparing for training camp, however, and so I never wound up finishing my degree in secondary education. I had more than enough credit hours to graduate, but I never completed the student-teaching requirements necessary to get my degree. That is something I regret terribly to this day, but I promised myself that I am going to finish that degree before I die. Maybe, when I finally graduate, they will induct me into the Wyoming Hall of Fame. I hope so. I am in the Missouri Hall of Fame, but I really want to get into Wyoming's, which apparently requires a degree. (Hopefully somebody on the selection committee will read this and help me out!) Of course, the College Hall of Fame is out because you need to be selected to play in one of the All-America games or be selected in one of the polls. Considering Shurmur was my coach at Wyoming and we had a 1–9 record, the chances of me making an All-American team were slim to none.

Later that summer, I packed up and moved to Evanston, Illinois, which was where the Cardinals held their preseason training camp. I remember getting there and being absolutely scared to death. I was totally outside my comfort zone, and I knew that I was going to have to prove myself all over again. The first thing we did was take physicals. I went in and the doctor ran me through some tests. Turn your head and cough...pee in a cup...yadda yadda yadda. I felt like a guinea pig in there, as a whole team of doctors took turns poking and prodding me. One of them would do something and then they would all huddle together to talk about it, whispering and pointing. I was so nervous that I thought I was going to throw up! When I was done, they told me that I had a heart murmur. And, if that wasn't bad enough, they also told me that my cholesterol level was through the roof!

We needed to get to the bottom of it, so they started questioning me about what I had been eating. I told them that I had spent the summer running and lifting weights and getting into shape. I also told them that the coaches wanted me to gain some weight, so I had been eating some extra food at my meals. Well, the fact of the matter was I had been eating ice cream night and day that summer at my parents' business. I would have milk shakes for breakfast, lunch, and dinner, followed by a big bowl of chocolate chip ice cream before bed. As a result, I had gone from 230 pounds up to 255 pounds in about two months, probably from nothing but ice cream!

Apparently, my health situation at the time was like a ticking time bomb. They immediately put me on a strict diet and then sent me down to St. Louis to take some stress tests. I was pissed! I didn't want to leave training camp at all, but they insisted. I was already behind the eight ball being a fifth-rounder, and I knew that I needed to be out there learning the playbook. I wound up missing the first two weeks of training camp. We were short on offensive linemen too, which meant that the veterans had to go both ways in the stifling August heat! They were getting no rest out there and they were just livid. I was supposed to be their replacement for all of those two-a-day practices, and instead of being out there, I was having my heart monitored in an air-conditioned rehab facility.

When I finally showed up to training camp in Evanston, the other players already hated my guts. It was like, "Welcome to the team, asshole!" I was ostracized right out of the gate, just like I had been back in school. There I was, playing in the National Football League, a first-class, professional organization of teams, leagues, coaches, trainers, and players, and I was getting hazed and abused! Those guys razzed the shit out of me during camp. I tried to laugh it off, but it was tough. The other offensive linemen would even try to sabotage me by telling me the wrong snap counts and the wrong blocking assignments at the line of scrimmage. I would make a mistake and then the coaches would make the offense run the entire play over again. The coaches were all over me. Another time some of the guys stole my playbook, which really screwed me because not only could I not learn the plays, I was threatened with a big fine by the coaches. I just couldn't catch a break.

Plus, I had to do all of the rookie initiation stuff too, like singing my school fight song in the middle of dinner…while I was holding my nuts! It was totally ridiculous. But as a rookie, you just had to grin and bear it. I really hated all of that garbage. Hazing to me was just bullshit. In my entire 10-year professional career, I never hazed a guy. Not once. Guys have enough to worry about, let alone being awoken at 3:00 in the morning to sing songs in their skivvies.

The two guys leading the charge against me in those early days were Dan Dierdorf and Tom Banks, who are today two of my dearest friends. But back then I absolutely detested them! They had both gone to big schools (Dan to Michigan and Tom to Auburn) and assumed that because I had gone to school at Wyoming that I was just a hayseed. They rode my ass mercilessly, "mooing" and "baa'ing" like cows and sheep whenever they saw me. They abused me mentally to the point that I really had a hard time concentrating on what the hell I was supposed to be doing out there. As a matter of fact, the mental abuse was so bad that I seriously thought about quitting, which would have been exactly what they wanted me to do. I just couldn't understand why these guys would be doing this to a fellow teammate. It really just didn't register to me. Why, when you are trying to build a team, would others try to degrade and run down their fellow teammates?

In retrospect, I think it was because they were afraid that I was going to take one of their jobs from them, and they also might have been a little jealous of the media coverage I was getting. You see, I had gotten some publicity in training camp because I would speak my mind to the media. I never responded to questions with just a "yes" or "no" answer. I would tell people exactly how I felt, which was not politically correct by any means. The reporters loved me though, because I gave them something interesting and compelling to write about. Well, apparently offensive linemen are not supposed to be in the limelight. I guess some people think that privilege is reserved exclusively for the quarterbacks and running backs.

To make matters worse, they gave all of the rookies these intelligence tests. Well, I aced them. One of the coaches complimented me in front of the whole team and basically said I was brilliant, which only added to my troubles. Once the other linemen heard that, it was all over. They couldn't wait to give me the wrong information in order to make me look bad in front of the coaches. Then, whenever I would screw up, I could hear them all laughing about how "brilliant" I was. It really sucked.

CUTTING MY TEETH WITH THE CARDINALS

Another thing that hurt my reputation was that a bunch of relatives in Chicago sent in a ton of "fan mail" for me on these postcards that were a part of some grocery store promotion or something. The cards said, "Conrad Dobler is No. 1 in our hearts and No. 66 in your program. We want to see more of him on the field." Well, they filled out like 5,000 of them and sent them in. One day I got to my locker and there were these huge mailbags full of postcards addressed to me. To my horror, all of the other linemen were sitting there reading them out loud and laughing. You see, we had an exhibition game with the Bears and I had gotten my relatives tickets, so they thought that they would try to help me out by telling the Cardinals that they were my fans and I was their favorite player. They meant well, but it made my life a living nightmare! The other players thought I was just an arrogant asshole.

I came into camp as an offensive lineman, but the Cardinals' coaches were trying me out at several different positions, including defensive end. I remember lining up across from Dan Dierdorf on some pass protection drills, and on several occasions I absolutely beat his ass, which really pissed him off. Here he is, this All-American from Michigan, getting beat by this nobody hick from Wyoming! I loved it. Well, he hated it, and it drove him nuts. He and Tom Banks, the center, then got together in the huddle to teach me a lesson. A few plays later those two ran a play, a fake-pass trap, where they double-teamed me and really let me have it. Dierdorf stood me up and Banks came down on me from my blind side and knocked me, ass over tea kettle, on my back. I didn't know what hit me. They both just looked down on me while I was laying there, and one of them said, "How do you like that, rookie?" I questioned why they ran a trap play during a pass rush drill. I came to believe that they were just both assholes. I spent a lot of time at training camp by myself because I was the only rookie on offense that season.

Even the offensive line coach, Bill Austin, thought it was funny. For some reason, he hated me, too! Maybe it was a rookie thing, I don't know.

We were reviewing defensive formations one day—over-and-unders, 4-3 and 3-4 formations, etc.—where Austin would show us pictures of defensive formations on the overhead projector and then quiz the linemen on what they were. Well, when it came to my turn, he flipped it on and then flipped it off, in like a nanosecond! I couldn't even see what it was. Then he asked me to identify it, which I couldn't, so he just started laying into me in front of the entire team. It was awful.

You know, because of Dierdorf, Banks, and Austin, I became really cynical. I just wasn't going to take any shit from anybody after dealing with those guys. In many regards, they helped to create the monster in me. After dealing with those assholes, I was like, "Fuck everybody." I wasn't going to take any crap from anybody, so I figured I was going to have to do whatever it took to take care of myself. If nobody was going to look out for me, then I was going to be as mean and nasty as I could be to protect myself. I fought every defensive player every day in practice after that and just refused to back down. Most offensive linemen are passive, but that just wasn't me. I was aggressive and took the battle to my opponent, which many perceived as being dirty. I played the offensive line with a defensive lineman's mentality.

I hung in there, and eventually I made it through training camp. I think my new attitude might have worn them down a little bit. Eventually they acknowledged my abilities, and so we were able to coexist. They still thought I was a real dipshit though. Coming into camp, I knew nothing about the NFL, and it really showed. I remember talking to Tom Banks one time and he was telling me something about the Washington Redskins and their star quarterback, Sonny Jurgensen. "Who the hell is that?" I asked. Tom said, "You have never heard of Sunny Jurgensen?" I said, "Jurgensen? Sure. The hand cream." He looked at me like I was a complete moron. He thought I was fucking with him, but I wasn't. I really had no idea. I had just never really followed professional football. As a kid, I never had time for it, and therefore it wasn't that important to me. Suddenly though, it was really important to me.

I played in some of the preseason games and figured I must have played well enough to make the 55-man roster. I remember the Saturday before our first game. We had a final walk-through practice. I had been so nervous about being cut that I actually counted out all 55 players in practice, just to make sure I was going to be there on the sideline the next day. After practice, one of the assistants told me that the head coach, Bob Hollway, wanted to see me in his office. I figured he wanted to personally congratulate me for making the team, or better yet maybe he wanted to tell me that I was starting, so I ran over to his office to talk to him.

I went into his office and he told me to sit down. He then proceeded to tell me that he was sorry, but I had gotten caught up in the numbers. I said, "Wait a minute, I am not following you. I just counted the number of players out there at practice and there were 55. What is the problem?" He then looked at me, smiled, and asked, "Did you remember to count yourself?" Oh shit, I forgot to count myself! I was number 56. So I walked out of there in a daze, wondering what in the hell just happened. Dierdorf later told me that when the other linemen heard I got cut, they all went out and drank beers to celebrate. Bastards!

Anyway, as I was cleaning out my locker one of the assistants told me to stay close by, just in case somebody got injured and they needed me. So I hung out for the next couple of days, laying low. I was living in an apartment at the time with three other rookies, and it was awkward, to say the least. After a few days of waiting around, I packed up my stuff and drove to Chicago to spend a few days with my relatives, the ones who had sent the postcards. I also knew a gal that lived there too, which was just what I needed to get my head cleared.

After a week of hanging out in the Windy City I figured my football career was all over. I decided to go back to Wyoming to finish my degree and become a teacher. I had given it my best shot and realized it just wasn't meant to be. Then, just as I was about to drive back to Laramie, I got a call from one of the assistants with the Cardinals. He told me that Chuck Hutchison, the team's starting right guard, had torn his knee up in the first game, and they needed me to rejoin the team. Unbelievable!

So I sped back to St. Louis to get fitted for equipment. Just like that, I was back in business. I was only cut from the team for eight days, and I only missed one game of the 1972 regular season. My first contract was for $17,500, plus a $5,000 signing bonus. I thought I had hit the lottery! When Dierdorf and the other linemen found out that I had returned from the dead, they were pissed. *Really* pissed. I was not looking forward to seeing those assholes in the locker room, but even in the face of adversity, I was determined to make the most of my opportunity. I suited up for practice and didn't say a word to anybody. I was just going to do my job and not make any waves. I studied my playbook and knew that I was prepared to go. The time off had been nice too, because I was well rested and ready to bang some heads.

On the depth chart, I was initially assigned as the reserve backup guard, and I was also assigned to play on all the special teams—kickoff, punt, extra point, and field goal. At least I knew I was going to get some time on the field with the special teams.

I will never forget being out on the field for the opening kickoff of my first pro game, the second regular-season game of that 1972 season, in Washington. It was almost surreal. To see all of the fans in that huge stadium and to be a part of the action was really exciting. I remember that I played okay that game, despite the fact that we lost 24–10. I worked hard during practice those next few weeks and tried to stay humble. I remember being physically exhausted every day after practice from battling with everybody. Come game time, though, I was ready to go.

In Week 5, we had to play Washington again, and this time they crushed us 33–3. The Redskins had a great team that year with an 11–3 record under George Allen and went on to win the NFC championship that year only to lose in the Super Bowl to the undefeated Miami Dolphins. Although I had planned on sitting on the bench during most of that game, I wound up getting to start on offense, which really blew me away. There was another guy in there, but apparently the coaches liked me better and wanted to give me a try.

So I got my first start and I also continued to play on all of the special teams. I even blocked a punt for a nine-yard loss, which was huge. After the game I was just drenched with sweat. I probably lost 20 pounds of water weight that day. I could hardly walk I was so tired. Dierdorf and Banks went to the coaches and told them that they needed me on the offensive line exclusively and that the team was wearing me out by having me play on all of the special teams. The coaches agreed.

That was a real turning point for me. To see Dan and Tom stick up for me almost brought tears to my eyes. I had finally earned their respect by working hard and being a team player, and that meant a lot to me. We got along after that, probably because they figured being a dick to me would only hurt the team, or they figured that I wasn't that bad of a guy. Of course, I still kept to myself. Either way, it was great to not have to worry about all of the petty politics. I remember feeling like I was officially a part of the group a few weeks later, after the *Monday Night Football* game in Miami in Week 11, when the guys invited me out for a beer with them. That was a big deal. Our trust grew and grew from there, and eventually we had each other's backs. We actually had become a pretty proficient offensive line toward the end of the year.

Overall, however, we were playing like shit, and by Week 13, we had not won since beating Minnesota in Week 4. But we finally got back in the win column toward the end of the year with a 24–14 win over the Rams. I remember that game for two reasons. First, I will never forget when our quarterback, Jim Hart, hit rookie wide receiver Bobby Moore for a 98-yard completion. (You may know Bobby as Ahmad Rashad, as he changed his name the following season.) Sadly, it would go down in the record books as the longest non-touchdown pass play in NFL history, a record that is impossible to break. The poor kid just ran out of gas at the 2-yard line. Second, I remember nearly being killed out there on the field because our grounds crew had used some new chemical to melt the ice on the frozen field. I think it must have been Agent Orange or something, because guys got bad burns from it. After the game, it sounded like a torture chamber from all the guys screaming as we tried to wash this stuff off in the showers.

We beat the Eagles that following week to end the season on a high note, but overall we had a pretty terrible season, going 4–9–1. As a result, the entire coaching staff got canned. The way they found out was pretty crazy, too. During halftime of that last game with Philly, our owner, Bill Bidwell, changed all the locks on the coaches' offices. After the game, the coaches couldn't even get into their own offices to retrieve their personal belongings. This was done to make sure that they couldn't take any playbooks or anything. (It's not like anyone would want them; we only won four games.) To be honest, I was happy as hell that Bob Hollway got the boot. None of us cared for the guy, and we were all ready for a change of leadership.

That off-season I drove back to Wyoming in my brand-new brown-and-gold Pontiac Firebird. It was my first big purchase, and it was sweet. I was all set to go back and finally finish my degree but got sidetracked, believe it or not, by my new car. I wound up getting into an accident that winter and the frame got bent pretty badly. It was so bad, in fact, that they said it was going to take a couple of months to fix it. So I went to work for a car dealership in Laramie instead of going back to school.

The guy who owned the dealership was a big Wyoming football booster and he was happy to help me out. They said that they would give me a demo car to drive, plus I figured I could make a few extra bucks. Well, it turned out that I was pretty damn good at it. I wound up selling about 35 cars a month and nearly made more that off-season than I did playing in the NFL that first year. I was their top sales guy by a mile. They begged me not to go back to St. Louis. Not knowing if I was going to have a job that next season with the new coaching staff that was coming in, I figured that selling cars would be my backup plan.

One of the friends I was hanging out with that off-season was a professor at the University of Wyoming. His girlfriend had young children, and there was a gal at the registrar's office that would babysit for them. I dropped him off one night and I met her when I went inside. Her name was Linda, and she was beautiful. We started talking, and I told my friend that I would drive her home for him. He took me aside and told me that even though I was pretty smooth with the ladies, there was no chance of me scoring with her. He told me that she was a single mom and was not interested in dating anybody. Well, I took that as a personal challenge. I hated to lose, especially with women. Long story short, I drove her home and we started dating. We got pretty serious that winter and things were going well. She had a two-year-old son, Mark, who I really liked a lot. We fell in love, and she decided to move out to St. Louis with me.

I remember meeting her ex-husband for the first time. He had joined the army and came to see Mark once when he was on leave. I stayed away to give him some space. Well, I came home and Linda was crying and really upset. She didn't get along with him and they had gotten into an argument over something. Seeing her so distraught really upset me, so I drove over to his hotel to talk to him. I knocked on his door and politely introduced myself. I told him that I was in love with Linda and that if we got married, I would like to adopt his son. I said that he had every right to see his son and that I would never stand in the way of him having a relationship with his son. He appreciated that.

I then told him that if he ever upset Linda again to the point that she started crying, I was going to break his legs. I got right up in his face and said that it was not a threat; it was a promise. Needless to say, that was the last I heard from the guy. I think he was just happy not to have to pay any more child support. So it all worked out in the end. He did give me his permission to adopt his son. Years later, Mark sadly found out that his dad had committed suicide. I don't think it had anything to do with me.

After a few months off I was looking forward to getting back out onto the field for training camp. We had a new head coach, Don Coryell, and I was excited to show him what I could do. I knew what to expect this time and had paid my dues, so to speak. When I got to camp, however, I learned about the unwritten rule that said a guy couldn't lose his job due to injury. Chuck Hutchison, the guy who got injured that season, was now healthy and ready to go. So I came into camp as a member of the second team, which really pissed me off. I wasn't mad at Chuck—he was a good enough guy and all—I was just mad at the situation. Chuck wasn't the type of player to make many mistakes. He was a second-round draft choice from Ohio State, and management certainly wanted to get their money's worth out of him as a starter. So I knew that it was going to be a long season. I was totally depressed and wondered whether or not I was ever going to get another opportunity to play again.

Our offensive line coach was a guy by the name of Jim Hanifan, and he took a liking to me. He could see that I was upset and told me to just keep my head up. He basically told me to hang in there and that he was going to do whatever he could to get me some action. I continued to work hard in practice and prepared like I was still going to be the starter. That was my mind-set. It's like that old saying, "Pride is hard to swallow, but it will go down." Well, one day during training camp we were having a scrimmage up in Minnesota against the Vikings. There were no kickoffs or anything like that in scrimmages; the teams just lined up to run plays. So the coaches yelled for the first team to get out there to run the offense. They all ran out there, but then Chuck came running back to the sideline yelling, "Does anybody have a chin strap? I lost mine."

Hanifan saw that, and he was pissed that Hutchison wasn't prepared for the first play of the scrimmage. So he looked right at me, sort of smiled, and said, "Get your ass in there." Believe it or not, Chuck lost his job right then and there. I was the starter from that point on. It was incredible. I felt bad for the guy, but that is just the way it goes sometimes. He never went on the field again after that with the Cardinals and wound up getting shipped off to Cleveland. I had this old adage about the six "Ps": Proper Preparation Prevents Piss-Poor Performance. Hutchison wasn't prepared on that particular play, and it cost him dearly.

While it really doesn't matter how Chuck lost his chin strap, I was able to take advantage of that tiny opportunity and I made the most of it. Because of that incident, for the last 35 years I have carried a chin strap with me in my briefcase as a reminder that life is precious, opportunities are often rare, and that overlooking simple details can really cost you. Opportunities come in all shapes and sizes, and I was in the right place at the right time and was prepared to capitalize on that opportunity. It always amazes me to think about how something as small and insignificant as a chin strap can change two people's lives so much. Beyond that, I also learned about how fragile your job was in the NFL, which was why I always played even when injured. In fact, from that moment on, I vowed never to come out of a game unless I was carried off, because I knew that somebody else was going to take my job. (For the record, no, I didn't steal Chuck's chin strap that day. Or did I? At my age, I just can't recall.)

Playing under Coryell was fun, and that was a first for me. Football had never really been fun for me in the past. It had been more about work and about the fear of failure. In high school I played just to get out of work; in college I played out of fear of losing my scholarship; and in my rookie season I was playing because it was my job. Now, however, I was settled in and I was playing for fun. What an amazing concept! I was actually having a good time out there.

I learned a ton working with Hanifan; the guy was a real visionary. He got us blocking in an entirely new system. In the old system, we would typically take two steps back and then take defensive linemen on as they came at us. In the new system, however, we charged straight at them right off the snap of the ball. He didn't want us to give up an inch. Today that type of blocking is commonplace, but back then it was a pretty radical philosophy. If executed correctly, it is very, very effective.

We had a really good offensive line. In addition to me at right guard, we had Dan Dierdorf at right tackle, Tom Banks at center, Bob Young at left guard, and Ernie McMillan at left tackle. Dierdorf and I developed some great chemistry out there together in the trenches. It was like we could read each other's minds after a while. We would switch up from man-to-man to zone coverage without even saying a word to each other. We just knew what the other guy was going to do in certain situations. If he went one way, I would automatically go the other. We were not only gelling as teammates on the field, we were also becoming good friends off the field, which was pretty neat.

I remember one night getting home late from a road game in Miami and just being hungry as hell. So Dierdorf, Banks, and I went out to Denny's. We had been drinking, and we were just starving. The waitress came over and asked what we wanted. We were too ornery to wait, so we just blurted out, "Bring us everything on the breakfast menu." Sure enough, she came back with about 50 entrees, and I'll be damned if we didn't eat every bit of it. We sat there eating pancakes and waffles and eggs and bacon, telling stories and just having a ball. We would do a lot of dumb stuff like that.

We were like the three musketeers, and we loved raising hell together. I remember being at training camp together that next year. We used to talk other guys into playing a drinking game called Cardinal Puff. We would go out to a local bar and line up tequila shots. The guys would then have to repeat things, sort of like the game Simon Says. If they screwed up, they would have to take a shot. Well, we had the bartender in on the fix, so we were actually drinking water instead of tequila. Sure enough, we would get these guys good and liquored up and then the next morning at practice they would be puking all over the place. It was pretty hilarious.

Dan and Tom and I would spend a lot of time in bars together, at home and on the road. Bars were our home away from home, where we could go and get away from it all. After a while, however, I started getting recognized, which could be a blessing as well as a curse. With the ladies, it was definitely a blessing but with the drunk guys, not so much.

Every now and then, some idiot full of liquid courage would come up to me and try to pick a fight. "You don't look so tough," he would say, just begging me to deck him. Well, I didn't want to deal with shit like that, nor the inevitable lawsuit which would follow, so I tried to diffuse those situations as quickly as possible. I would either buy them a drink or walk away. Sometimes, if they were persistent, I would say, "If you want me to fight you, then you are going to have to write me a check, because I don't fight anyone for free. Fighting is part of my job, and right now I am off duty." That usually pacified them.

Well, we wound up with an identical 4–9–1 record that year, but we had some significant wins that season, and we could tell that we were on the verge of turning the corner as a team. We played in the toughest conference in those days, the Eastern Division of the NFC, along with the Dallas Cowboys, Washington Redskins, Philadelphia Eagles, and New York Giants. We had some great rivalries between those teams and we lost some close games that year. Coryell hated to lose and would do whatever it took to gain an edge, especially against the Redskins, his arch enemies.

Don *hated* the Redskins. Their coach, George Allen, was an espionage freak, which made our lives a living hell the weeks we played them. Don had us taking buses to different practice fields every day, just in case George had spies camped out somewhere trying to steal our plays. There was this big building across the street from Busch Stadium, and one time Don saw a guy in a window watching us practice. He thought it was George up there filming us, so he sent some guys up there to interrogate the perpetrator. Of course it wasn't someone from the Redskins, but Don and George were so paranoid about each other it was almost insane. Trust me, had they been able to afford it, they would have had satellites up there watching each other.

Stealing plays has always been a part of the game. Everybody is looking for an edge. I don't care if it is in business or in football or in raising your kids or even in romance, everybody wants to get ahead. Those who are able to find that edge are usually the ones who are the most success-ful. Now, whenever you cross the line and go too far to gain that edge, that is when it all comes tumbling down. That was the case for all the Wall Street brokers who have lost millions these past few years, and it was also the case for Bill Belichick in New England with the whole "Spygate" thing. They cheated and they got nailed.

Coryell was an interesting guy. He was always looking for new and interesting ways to motivate us and to get us ready to play. One of the things that really drove him crazy was whenever we had to play against a team in really cold weather. I remember preparing for a big home game against the Redskins one time. It was a record cold spell and the tem-perature wasn't going to be above freezing for the game. So he had us practicing outside all week to get acclimated. He then decides to give us this big Vince Lombardi–style pep talk to get us all fired up.

He starts by telling us about the Alaska Pipeline and about how the native Eskimos could work much longer hours in the cold than the workers from the lower 48 states. He said all kinds of tests were done on them to figure out why they could work so long in the bitter cold with such little rest or even protective clothing. The tests came back inconclusive, and it was determined that it was all psychological, a simple case of mind over matter. The workers from the lower 48 states would simply psych themselves out by thinking too much about the cold. As a result, they couldn't work very long without taking breaks to warm up. He then drew the correlation about how we were going to be mentally ready for the cold, whereas the Redskins would be psyched out. "You're used to it," he said, "and that is why you are going to kick their asses."

Meanwhile, Dierdorf was sitting next to me and we were both crack-ing up over this whole thing. He then raised his hand, and asked Don a real serious question: "Don, what you have said makes sense. But what happens if I get into my stance tomorrow and look across that line into the face mask of the defensive lineman across from me and I see an

Eskimo?" Everybody burst out laughing. Everybody, that is, except Coryell. He got serious and almost worried and said, "You know, you're right, I wouldn't put it past Allen for a minute, to have a team of Eskimos. That no good, cheatin' son of a bitch."

Coryell was just obsessed with the game. He had that angry, pissed-off look about him when he was on the sideline, like he had just eaten a dead rat. He was consumed with coaching. He loved to win and he hated to lose. He lived it and breathed it. That was all he wanted to do in life. He was always on a quest to find a way to beat the other team. Football was chess to Don; he loved the tactics and the strategy. I loved that type of attitude, and it trickled down to the rest of us. We knew that this guy was going to do whatever it took to win, so we got in line right behind him.

Hanifan was great, too. He would even give us written tests before each game. Some guys hated it, but I loved that stuff. I wanted to learn and become a student of the game. I would study our game plan incessantly, just reading it and reading it, memorizing every little detail I could. I didn't want any "M.A.s," or missed assignments. Vince Lombardi, the legendary coach of the Packers, wrote in his book about one of his teams that had an offensive line that went an entire season without a single M.A. That was incredible to me, almost impossible. But that's what I aspired to. Hell, that was a statistic that our entire offensive line could shoot for. As a lineman, the only time you ever got noticed out there was when you fucked up. So I wanted to do everything I could do to *not* get noticed.

The 1974 season almost never got started because of a labor dispute between the players and the owners. Dierdorf was the team's union representative, so we sort of bonded during that time while we were out on the picket line during training camp. We became pretty tight friends after that and our friendship only grew from there. Once the strike was settled, we hit the field and had a great season, going 10–4. In the process we became one of the best pass-protecting offensive lines in the league. In fact, that season we led the entire NFL by allowing a league-low 16 sacks. As a unit, we were just dominant.

We even made the playoffs that year, but sadly lost in the first round 30–14 in Minnesota. I remember it being colder than hell up there, and the field was iced over with a lot of glare, very similar to the famous "Ice Bowl," the 1967 NFL Championship Game between Green Bay and Dallas. But it was significant for me personally because it was during the Vikings game that the legend of me being a dirty player got started. Midway through the game I got into a tussle with Vikings defensive tackle Doug Sutherland. We had played Minnesota about a month earlier, and he had tried to stomp on my nuts during one play while I was on the ground. So there was some bad blood there, and we were going at it pretty hard that night. Anyway, after the game, Doug said that I had bitten him while we were going at it down in the trenches.

Well, that was total bullshit, but the media ran with it. They asked me about it afterward, and I threw it back at them by simply asking, "What the hell were Sutherland's fingers doing in my face mask?" You want to talk about being a cheap shot; that guy was trying to gouge my goddamn eyes out, for crying out loud. Looking back, I never denied it, nor did I confirm it. I just couldn't believe that someone was saying something as stupid as that. Well, the horse was out of the barn after that, and my reputation for playing dirty became larger than life.

The media played it up like I was a vampire, and some fans even came out with wooden stakes and heads of garlic. It was pretty hilarious. Hey, I was an opportunist, so I just ran with it. The funny thing is Doug later admitted that he made the whole damn thing up. I guess he wanted it off of his conscience before he wound up on his deathbed. Safe to say that 35 years later, I am over it. (It's okay, Doug; I forgive you.) But to this day, I get people coming up to meet me and saying, "You're not going to bite me, are you?"

I had actually gotten bit myself one time as a rookie, by Dallas linebacker Lee Roy Jordan. I choke-blocked him during a game and put him on his back. (Choke-blocking is a blocking scheme involving a pivot step and a slow second step to block the defender.) While we were down on the ground, my fist got caught up under his chin strap. Pissed off about being taken down, he bit my thumb. It didn't hurt or anything because not only did I have it taped up at the time, but it turned out he didn't have any teeth. So technically he didn't bite me, he "gummed" me. I just figured that was a part of the game. The point is, I figured if you are going to get your fingers up in somebody's face, then you had better be prepared for the consequences. Anyway, I am glad that we can finally put Doug's urban legend to bed all these years later.

From there, the legend of me being a dirty player just grew and grew until it took on a life of its own. For instance, there is another incident from that 1974 season that I still get asked about: when I supposedly sucker-punched Giants rookie tackle Jim Pietrzak in the throat after the game when he tried to shake my hand. Well, it didn't quite happen that way. There were still two seconds left on the clock, so the game wasn't *technically* over yet. So when he extended his hand to offer me a congratulatory handshake, I nailed him. It was a real snot-bubbler, too. The guy was stunned. When the final whistle blew a moment later, I extended my hand. Now he was even more stunned. Hey, as long as time was still on the clock, I was not going to concede. If anything, I taught that rookie a valuable lesson about playing hard right up until the final whistle. Well, the media ran with it, and one thing I have found out is that once you have a reputation with the media, you are guilty until proven innocent. Even if you are innocent, you might remain guilty in the press because it makes for a better story.

I never really understood the whole "playing dirty" thing, to tell you the truth. Sure, I played mean and nasty, and sure I tried to knock guys on their asses. But I never deliberately went out to try to hurt anyone. That was not me. I battled and did whatever I could to win, but there is a difference between playing hard and trying to injure someone. I really enjoyed running downfield and looking for guys who were standing around. As an offensive lineman, you were always being abused. Defensive tackles were always pounding on you, so when the opportunity presented itself to take somebody down, you took it. I didn't try to be dirty; I just took advantage of opportunities when they presented themselves. If a guy was standing near a pile and the whistle hadn't blown yet, I was going to nail him. And if I didn't, Dierdorf would. That was our mentality.

We wanted to intimidate our opponents to get them thinking about us, rather than thinking about doing their jobs. It was a premeditated tactic, and it worked. Once I had gotten a reputation for being nasty, guys would come after me day in and day out and let me have it. Shit, I even wore shin pads on the back of my calves because of all the leg whips I gave. Hey, I could dish it out, but I could take it, too. I didn't complain. Most of the time I was just retaliating for what they were doing to me. I didn't call it "dirty." I called it "victim precipitated violence." What comes around goes around, in life and in football. Sometimes, karma is a real bitch.

That off-season I took a leap of faith and asked Linda to marry me. The timing was right. The wedding wasn't anything too fancy, but I figured after living together for the past year it was the least I could do to make an honest woman out of her and a respectable man out of me. Plus, we had her son Mark to think about. I adopted him, which officially made me a daddy. I have never referred to him as my stepson, though. I raised him, and he is my son. Anyway, I was really happy. We were living in a townhouse in suburban St. Louis, two houses down from my linemate Tom Banks and his wife. Tom and I would drive to practice every day and we became great friends. Linda and his wife became close too, which was really nice. Life was good.

The next four seasons were pretty incredible for me. I really refined my game and turned out to be a pretty damn good football player. I wound up getting voted to play in the Pro Bowl in 1975, 1976, and 1977, which was a huge honor because it was the coaches who voted me in, not the players who do the voting today. The coaches might have hated me, but they voted for me because I was the top right guard in the league during those years. As soon as the players started voting, I didn't have a prayer. My reputation for being dirty wouldn't allow for it, and besides, I kicked most of their asses.

We had some good teams in those days, as evidenced by the fact that one year we had nine players go to the Pro Bowl. The reason we never made it to any Super Bowls was pretty much summed up by the fact that eight of those nine players were on offense. At times our defense was brutal. Sorry guys, but it was true. We scored a lot of points but we gave up just as many. Our quarterback was Jim Hart and he was pretty darn good. We had good chemistry all the way around and for the most part we all liked each other. Coryell pushed us really hard, but we liked him as a coach, so we worked hard for him.

I remember getting an award one time with the rest of my line-mates for being named the top offensive line in the league. It was in Milwaukee, and I was there along with Dierdorf, Tom Banks, and Roger Finnie (Bob Young couldn't make it for some reason). So we're at this big dinner gala, and Milton Berle was the master of ceremonies. He was introducing us to this huge audience and he said, "There are only four of you here, where is the other guy?" Dierdorf then hollered out, "He heard you were going to be here M.C.'ing tonight." It was at that moment that I learned a very valuable lesson: never argue with a comedian when he has the microphone. Milton proceeded to abuse poor Dan for the rest of the evening. "You big, fat Neanderthal, are you going to eat all of the food in here? Or are you going to leave some for us?" It was pretty hilarious. I was just about to say something at the time too, but luckily Dierdorf beat me to it. For once, I was glad I kept my big mouth shut.

One of the other things I remember about that night was getting together with two twins who had posed for *Playboy*. Man, that was something else. That was the night I got my reputation for being a stud with my teammates, which was kind of cool, but I fooled around on my wife. I am not proud of it, but I did what I did. It is out there and I am not going to deny it.

After a while I knew that if I was going to have success at a high level, I was going to have to get bigger. We had some strong guys on our team and I did not want to be the weak link. So that off-season I joined a health club in Laramie. I was in pretty good shape and enjoyed jogging, which was tough at 7,000 feet above sea level, but I knew that I needed to get stronger. There weren't any other professional athletes in town to work out with, so I wound up training with some Mexican bodybuilders. They were the ones who taught me how to lift weights and how to get stronger. Eventually I was able to bulk up to around 280 pounds, which really helped me. I had always been naturally strong, but adding that extra mass allowed me to do some things out there that I had not previously been able to do.

When I got back to camp that summer, everybody thought that I had taken steroids, because I was ripped. Steroids were just starting to show up on the radar at that time, and some of the guys were already taking them. Nobody really knew how bad they were for you in those days. Thankfully, I never took any steroids. Ever. For steroids to be effective, you had to lift weights all the time. Well, I wasn't interested in working out four hours a day, so they didn't interest me. Had I taken them, they would have just made me fat.

My roommate Bob Young, however, took massive amounts of them. Hell, I used to have to inject him in the ass. He was the strongest man in the league at the time, no question. In fact, he even won the "Strongest Man in the NFL" contest when he lifted like 2,000 pounds on four lifts: dead lift, clean and jerk, bench press, and squat. The guy was just massive. The way he worked out was crazy, too. I remember watching him squat 600 pounds while he was smoking a cigarette. Sadly, Bob died in 1995 at the age of 52. He was a great guy, but there was a reason he died so young. He abused his body with steroids, and that ultimately cost him his life. It was a real tragedy. I'm sure the massive amount of weight he carried didn't help either.

A lot of guys took steroids in those days but not nearly to the extent that the players do today. These guys today are giants. I am a big guy for Christ's sake, but I look like a midget next to some of the players today. It is ridiculous. Look, steroids have been around for a long, long time. How do we know who did and didn't take them going back 50 or 100 years? We don't. So instead of calling this the "steroid era," I prefer to call this the "steroid-testing era." They need to come up with a better method of testing for it though, because the athletes who use them are about 10 steps ahead of the curve. The bottom line in my eyes is that it's cheating. I know, it's hard for you to accept me saying the word *cheating*, but get over it. If a guy gets caught, I don't feel sorry for him. Guys know damn well what they are putting in their bodies. But the system forces you to make a choice: do you want to keep your job, or do you want to get cut because you're not big enough?

Off the field, I studied my playbook whenever I could. I had become a student of the game. I wanted to learn everything I could about the opponents I would go up against each week. I watched game films constantly. I wanted to know which finger my opponent used to pick his nose and which hand he jerked off with. I wanted to know every little detail. I tried to find his tendencies and weaknesses so that I could exploit them. I looked at how he adjusted his stance, which way he leaned in certain situations, and where his eyes were looking. I really honed in on what he was trying to do, so that I could counter it and take him to the ground. I became obsessed with beating my opponent.

I remember playing Minnesota one time. They had the best defense in the league in those years, and their best player was defensive tackle Alan Page, leader of the vaunted "Purple People Eaters." I was a fierce competitor and I enjoyed going up against the very best, and at that time Alan was *the* guy. He was a monster and really quick off the ball. He had beaten me several times the last time we played the Vikings, so I went back and studied the film on him over and over. Eventually Tom Banks and I were able to figure out why he was getting such a good jump off the ball: he was keying in on Banks' fingers while he snapped the ball. Whenever Tom was about to snap it to the quarterback, his fingertips would turn white. Alan would key in on it, like a tell in poker, and get past him before the ball was even in the quarterback's hands. So, once Tom and I became aware of this, Tom was able to get Page to jump off-sides several times by just flinching his thumb as a decoy. Little things like that went a long way, and once we were able to figure that stuff out, we really capitalized on it.

I wound up playing in St. Louis for six seasons, and during that time our offensive line pretty much dominated. We led the league in fewest sacks allowed for four straight seasons. Our best year was probably 1975, when we only gave up eight sacks the whole year, tying San Francisco for the record at the time. There weren't a lot of stats to recognize offensive linemen at the time, so we wanted that recognition. It was a pride thing for us. As linemen we took great pride in the fact that our quarterback had a lot of time to throw the ball. In 1975 Jim Hart threw for 19 touchdowns and more than 2,500 yards. Shit, to put into perspective just how good our offensive line was, Jim Otis led the NFC in rushing that year with more than 1,000 yards, and he was a slow, fat, white guy. How's that for productivity?

A lot of pretty important people have said that we were one of the best offensive lines ever to play in the NFL, and I would certainly have to agree with that statement. Our core group stayed together for five seasons, which was the key. We all spent many hours becoming students of the game, and we developed an intense sense of team pride and a desire to not let the other guys on our team down. Nowadays, with all of the free agency, you don't see stuff like that as much.

When it was all said and done, we finished the 1975 season with a pretty damn good 11–3 record, and we won the NFC Eastern Division. We had a great team that year. We started out slow but then won nine of our last 10 games. A lot of people had us pegged to win it all, but we were beaten in the first round of the playoffs by the Rams 35–23 out at the

Coliseum in Los Angeles. What I remember most about that game was my feud with Rams defensive tackle Merlin Olsen. He and I had become archrivals over the past couple of years, and it all boiled over that afternoon in Los Angeles.

Merlin was a 14-time Pro Bowl player who thought I was a dirty, cocky, 25-year-old punk kid who needed to be taught a lesson. I, on the other hand, thought he was an old, fat, pompous windbag. Well, I went out there and I embarrassed him. I mean, I just kicked his ass up one side of the field and down the other. It was brutal. I was knocking him five yards off the ball. He couldn't even get off the line of scrimmage on a pass rush. If you wanted to see him on the instant replay after I blocked him, you had to go into the kitchen because I knocked him so far off the screen. I dominated him so badly that he took himself out of the game and walked off the field in the fourth quarter. Even though we lost that game, it was probably the most memorable game of my career. After the game Olsen was so mad at me that he said to a reporter, "One of these days someone is going to break Dobler's neck, and I am not going to send any flowers."

That 1975 season was also the first season I was selected to play in the Pro Bowl, held in the Superdome in New Orleans, and the feud between me and Olsen really accelerated then. The Rams' coaches seemed to always coach in the Pro Bowl, because that honor goes to the team that loses in the conference championship game. They always lost in the conference title game, so Chuck Knox had a lot of opportunities to coach the Pro Bowl. Anyway, I was getting my ankles taped in the trainer's room before a practice, and there were three or four Rams players in there, including Jack Youngblood and Hacksaw Reynolds. Then Merlin walked in. I figured that, since we were all teammates for the week, there wouldn't be any problems. Olsen then came over and said to me, "You know what Dobler? The next time we play you I'm going to kick you right in the nuts." I just looked at him and smiled and said, "Get a ticket and get in line Merlin, because for a long time a lot of people have been trying to take me down. Good luck." The trainer taping my ankle thought that a rumble was going to break out at that point, and he was nervous as hell. I remember seeing a whirl of white tape spinning around my ankle and then him practically sprinting out of the room.

Did he think because of my tough-guy reputation, I was going to jump off the table and take a swing at Olsen? What was I really supposed to do? The other Rams players were kind of laughing and giggling. Why would he have made a comment like that? I couldn't believe he had taken what had happened in the course of a game personally. That's football. You don't like the way a guy plays? That's fine. Don't bitch about it, just go out there and do your job. I always found that odd, how guys took stuff like that with them off the field. It wasn't personal to me. What I did out on the field had nothing to do with who I was. When the game was over, it was over. I didn't hate anybody personally. I wasn't out to embarrass guys; I just wanted to win. Olsen, however, made it personal.

During that week at the Pro Bowl, Merlin and I really went at it. Pro Bowls are supposed to be exhibition games where very little defense is played. They don't want guys to get hurt, so there is an unwritten rule that no one goes 100 percent out there. Well, he and I battled each other during practice every day. We would still go at it even after the whistle. It was fun. After a while all of the other players would just back up and watch us beat on each other. It got pretty intense. Luckily we were on the same team, because I think I might have tried to kill the guy.

The funny thing about it is that years later, I was still on old Merlin's mind. That tickled me. You see, after the guy retired he got into acting and wound up getting his own TV show called *Father Murphy*, a family-friendly program in which he played the patriarch of an orphanage. In one episode there was a cemetery scene in which he had a gravestone that read: "CONRAD DOBLER. GONE, BUT NOT FORGIVEN." How funny is that? Here is a Hall of Famer who has become an incredibly successful businessman, owned car dealerships, was a broadcaster for NBC, and has probably made more money than God, yet I was still on his mind. Hey

Merlin, let the grudge go, pal. Get over it; it's been 35 years. I also chuckle when I think back to his comment about "not sending me flowers" when I died. How ironic is it that he became the national spokesperson for FTD, pushing flowers? Classic.

I tried to use intimidation as a tactic, absolutely. Dierdorf used to say, "It was like 10 of us playing a football game and then there is Dobler, who was in a bar-room brawl with the guy across from him." That was my mentality. If you could take your opponent out of his game and make him more concerned about you than he was about his responsibilities out on the field, that was mission accomplished. If guys spent their time trying to beat up on me, rather than focusing on tackling our ball carrier, that was fantastic. I would take that abuse because it was helping my team. I didn't care what my opponents thought of me; I only cared about my teammates.

By then I had decided to use my reputation to my advantage. I played with an edge and certainly wouldn't take any bullshit from any defensive linemen. I was going to use whatever means necessary to beat my opponent out there; that was how I was wired. I would try to distract him, attack him personally, and just abuse him any way I could. It was war when I went out there. For instance, if a defensive lineman jumped up in the air to try to deflect a pass, I would go right for his solar plexus. "Go ahead donkey," I would say. "I would just love a cut of those country ribs." That would bring their hands down immediately. I didn't want them tipping any balls from my quarterback, so I was going to do whatever I could to prevent that from happening. That was my job.

Believe it or not, opposing coaches used to do most of the ground work for me. They would talk with their defensive linemen before we played to warn them about my rough style and get them all riled up. I was already in their heads before the game even started. They were ready for me. It was now an ego thing with them, because they weren't about to take any shit from me. Meanwhile, I would go out and do my job, and because they were so worried about me and about what I may or may not try to do to them, they weren't focusing on doing their jobs. What a wonderful sight: to block a guy who is so desperate to beat my brains out, and then to see my running back run right past him and into the end zone. Some of them got so pissed that they would just lose it. Such was the case for Oakland Raiders coach John Madden, who once put a bounty on my head. What pissed me off the most about it was not the fact that he put a bounty on me, but rather the reward: $100. Shit, John, I was worth at least 10 times that much.

Intimidation took many forms, but I was not a trash talker. To me that was bush-league stuff. Plus, I didn't want to waste my breath yapping at some idiot; I was too damn tired to begin with. So when guys started flapping their gums at me, I would just smile and wink at them. I was a firm believer that if you were going to talk the talk, then you had better be able to walk the walk. Again, it was "victim precipitated violence," meaning I would play guys straight up until they started getting dirty on me. The first time I got poked in the eye or punched in the nuts, the gloves came off. If guys wanted to play dirty, then that was fine with me. I could leg whip, chop block, or punch them in the solar plexus. I might come at a guy with a hard forearm to his chin or to his esophagus to soften him up. I never started out to injure anyone, but if a guy tried to hurt me, then I was going to try to hurt him. That was my livelihood, and I wasn't about to just sit there and get disrespected. No way. It was my job to make sure the defensive linemen across from me wound up on the ground. Period. So I would do whatever I could to put them there. I was very good at my job, and my teammates appreciated that.

As far as retaliation went, we took that pretty seriously. We even kept a little black book of guys who took cheap shots on our teammates. We had a list, particularly of guys who were in our division—the Cowboys, Redskins, Eagles, or Giants—who we knew we could get back the next time we saw them. The beauty of playing offensive line was that once the ball was past the line of scrimmage, I could go hunt and destroy. The defensive guys were constantly chasing the ball carrier, whereas we were out there looking to nail guys. I would love getting back at dirty players like that, chasing them down and ear-holing them—*wham!*— when they least expected it. That was like having a grenade go off in your ear; you couldn't hear anything for five minutes.

On the flip side, interceptions were frightening times because that is when the defense gets to come after you. Those guys love nothing better than to flip unsuspecting offensive linemen upside down in those situations, so I always kept my head on a swivel. Guys would especially come looking for me in those instances, praying for an opportunity to lay a cheap shot on me. One interception in particular stands out. It was during a game against the Redskins at RFK Stadium in Washington. Wide receiver Mel Gray and I gave chase to this speedy little defensive back who had picked off Hart, but we couldn't catch him. As Gray got near the end zone, he got nailed on a vicious clip and went flying into a bunch of wooden folding chairs that were set up along the sideline. He was so pissed that he grabbed a chair and started swinging it at the guy who hit him. Before long all hell broke loose. I dove in to try to help him out and in the process I got blindsided and knocked to the turf. While I was down on the ground, I grabbed a broken chair leg and started whacking the toes and shins of the Redskins players who were trying to maim me. It was like a scene out of a movie, just crazy.

You know, NFL Films always shows this one particular play to illustrate just how dirty I was, where I am stepping on the head of a Giants defensive lineman. If you look closely at the footage, however, what you don't see is that this guy was going for my knees. That was the reason I stepped on his head; not to be dirty, but because he had just tried to take my knees out. Hey, I have always said "If you are man enough to give a cheap shot, then you had better be man enough to take one." Believe me, I took my fair share of cheap shots. I have a total of seven artificial knee transplants over the years to prove it.

I remember playing for Buffalo when a guy from New Orleans came at me on the first play of the game and knocked me on my ass. He then said a few things to me that I didn't appreciate. So on the very next play, when he tried to get by me with a rip move, I pinned his arm underneath mine and just fell to the turf. As I did, his arm snapped. Now, did I mean to break his arm? No. I wanted to hurt him and teach him a lesson, sure. But I never wanted to injure somebody to the point where they couldn't earn a living. There is a difference.

On a personal note, things were going well. Linda and I had settled into a groove and we were enjoying our life together. We did a lot with the other linemen and their wives, too. On Fridays we would all go out to dinner and a movie. It was sort of a pregame ritual for us. Those were neat times. We were close on the field and off the field. I think that Coryell encouraged that closeness in us. He was pretty intense between the white lines, but after practices he wanted us to hang out and build chemistry together. We were a really tight group.

My work ethic really helped me. I never got tired out there, and even if I was exhausted, I wouldn't tell anyone. I would stay in there and do my thing. I just kept grinding and grinding. That was the secret to my success. I was resourceful, too. My job was to get my guy down on the ground and out of the play. If I couldn't get a guy down one way, then I would find another way to get the job done. My blocking technique wasn't always fundamentally correct, but I was able to adapt and get the job done.

I learned a lot from playing next to Dierdorf; the guy was an amazing player. He was by far the best drive blocker in our day, and maybe the best to ever play the game. He was that good. Nobody could stop him. I once watched a defensive lineman put his shoulder on the ground to try to get underneath him and drive him back, and Dan countered by getting even lower and getting his face in the dirt. He came up under the guy and ultimately put him on his back. It was one of the most incredible things I have ever seen on a football field. It was beautiful. The guy was not only as strong as an ox, he was one hell of a smart player. A lot of people thought that New England guard John Hannah was the best ever, but I would argue that Dan was even better.

We nearly made it back to the playoffs in 1976 after posting a 10–4 record, but got passed up by our divisional rivals Washington and Dallas. What I remember most about that season was a preseason game in Tokyo. What a wild trip that was. We drank ungodly amounts of sake and got into a lot of trouble. It was wonderful. We wanted to experience the local culture and customs, so a bunch of us even visited a geisha house. The geisha girls definitely got their money's worth that night. I even learned a few new tricks. Hey, when in Rome, right?

Another highlight came late in the season when we beat the Rams 30–28 out in L.A. I had been looking forward to my much-anticipated rematch with Merlin Olsen. We went at it all game and it was brutal. I wanted to embarrass him and I did, but not before nearly being maimed. On one play in particular, he held me up by my shoulder pads only to have his linemate, Jack Youngblood, come barreling down to take my knees out. Luckily I saw him coming out of the corner of my eye and was able to turn just enough to avoid what would have probably been a career-ending injury. I was so pissed. I turned around and immediately kicked Jack square in the face. The sonofabitch deserved it. Merlin and I continued to battle all afternoon. One reporter said it "made a dog fight look like a square dance." Merlin retired after that season, and I was just glad that I wouldn't have to face him anymore. Good riddance.

We were all pretty upset about not making it back to the playoffs. We had beaten the Giants in our final game out at the Meadowlands, but we needed Dallas to beat Washington in the final game of the year in order to get in. We actually found out our fate as we were flying home from New York from the captain of the plane, who was giving us a play-by-play over the loudspeaker. We were rooting like hell for Dallas, but the Cowboys just couldn't get it done. Both teams made the playoffs anyway, so it was sort of a meaningless game for them. What a buzzkill that was, to learn our season was over in midair. Guys just started drinking at that point, since it was all over.

After the Pro Bowl in Seattle, I flew to Sarasota, Florida, to participate in the "Superstars" competition. It was this made-for-TV event where all these athletes from different sports were brought in to compete against each other. We spent a week doing all these crazy events such as rowing, track and field, swimming, cycling, and running an obstacle course. It was stressful to compete against all of those people with the cameras rolling. I remember bowling like a 240 in practice and then was unable to break 100 during the live taping. I was so nervous that I was practically throwing the ball down the lane as hard as I could. I wound up winning the clean-and-jerk title in the weight lifting competition. In the end I won a few bucks, and I didn't humiliate myself too badly, which was the most important thing. It was a lot of fun to be there and to be recognized as a sort of celebrity. Most importantly, I was able to get my mind off of football for a while, which was like therapy.

My last year in St. Louis was the 1977 season. Things went downhill that year, both on and off the field. Off the field, Linda and I were going through some ups and downs and it all sort of came to a head that off-season. Linda and I had a house in Wyoming, and when it came time for Mark to start the first grade, we decided it would be better for him to go there rather than in St. Louis. That way he wouldn't have to split up his school year between two cities. So he and Linda stayed in Laramie without me for the season and I moved to St. Louis. In so doing, I took a sort of sabbatical from my marriage.

It sounds kind of crazy, but we were going through a rough patch and I felt like I needed some space. I had met Linda right after my rookie year and was regretting not being able to live the rock star life that so many other professional athletes were living. I wanted an opportunity to sow my oats. Begrudgingly, she gave me that opportunity. She figured I was going to do what I was going to do either way, so she just told me to do it and get it out my system. She knew that I was either going to come back or I wasn't, and that was okay with her. We even went and told her folks what we were going to do, which was tough. They were pretty religious people and that was difficult for them. We convinced each other that we were living in different places for Mark's benefit, but deep down we knew the real reason: I was being selfish.

Tom Banks was getting a divorce at that time, so we both took full advantage of our newly found freedom. His nickname was "Wolf Man" because he had this huge bushy beard. What a great guy. We went out a lot that year and got into a lot of mischief. I messed around with a few girls and did some things I am not too proud of, but it is what it is. Drugs were pretty prevalent in the NFL at the time too, especially cocaine and marijuana. Hey, I was a child of the '60s, what more can I say? Tommy wound up getting into that stuff more than I did, which he paid a price for, but that was his decision. We all make mistakes and we all do things that we wish we could take back later in life. We went out drinking and partying every night we could. It was insane. Strip bars, clubs, restaurants, we did it all.

Celebrity is a fascinating thing. I remember one summer being out in Wyoming and attending a booster club party for the school's football team. We were in this big bar and there were a whole bunch of good-looking young ladies running around. Nobody really knew who I was, so nobody bothered to stop and talk to me. I was invisible. Later in the evening, the lead singer of the band that was playing announced that I was there, introducing me as a star NFL player. Within five minutes there were 10 ladies who came over to sit down and talk to me and my group of friends. It was incredible. It was at that moment, however, when I realized that it wasn't me that they were interested in, this supposed good-looking, handsome guy with the gift of gab; it was what I did for a living that they were interested in. It was all about what I did and how much I made, not who I really was. Believe it or not, I was so depressed from my little revelation that I just went back to my room and went to bed. Talk about enlightening.

On the field, meanwhile, something happened during training camp that year that had a pretty profound impact on my life. That July I wound up on the cover of *Sports Illustrated* with the caption "Pro Football's Dirtiest Player." There I was, on the bible of sports magazines for the whole world to see. "Dirty" would be the adjective that would forever be linked to me. I didn't know how significant it was at the time, to tell you the truth. I had done some articles with some other publications in the past—*Inside Sports*, *The Sporting News*, and *Sport* magazine—but this was different. It was the first time an offensive lineman had ever made the cover, and it was a pretty big deal. Now everybody knew who I was, and I had a big target on my back. It wasn't like I wanted to be known as the dirtiest player in football though. Who in their right mind would want that moniker? Not me, but that was how I was labeled. So I dealt with it. Shit, I embraced it.

One positive was that even though a lot of offensive linemen thought I was an asshole and were jealous of my success, they now appreciated the fact that I was getting the position a lot of publicity and notoriety. Several big-time players would later tell me that they really appreciated it because they were now getting interviewed by the media and gaining more respect. I took that as quite a compliment because when I first got in the league, reporters never talked to the offensive linemen unless we got a big holding penalty called on us or something like that. So from that perspective it was kind of neat. If anything, I would hope that in some small way my legacy is tied into helping to promote the image of offensive linemen, for better or for worse.

Before long I was doing national TV interviews and getting a lot of attention. One week CBS sent Phyllis George to interview me for their *NFL Today* show. They set us up in a local jail cell, for dramatic effect I suppose. Hell, I didn't care. They could call me a criminal all they wanted to; I was just excited about being seen on national TV sitting next to the former Miss America. What a knockout!

So I went out and bought a brand-new pair of Levis for the occasion. The interview was scheduled to follow our practice, and I was pretty uptight. I didn't want anything to go wrong. After practice I really got dolled up because I wanted to look extra special for Phyllis. I first put on my flowered silk shirt and then grabbed my new Levis. The first leg went on smooth, and the second leg…shit, there was no second leg. Dammit, somebody had cut off the other leg.

I was pissed, so I started throwing things and tipping over lockers. Guys were running for their lives. Dierdorf and Jackie Smith came running over and offered me their pants. I was grateful for the gesture. I first tried on Dan's but they were huge; you could have fit two people in those things. Jackie's, meanwhile, were about two sizes too small. But I was desperate and was about to go on the air, so I took them. I just made sure not to bend over too far during the interview, otherwise they might've split right up the ass. Phyllis asked me, "Conrad, how do you plead to charges that you are the meanest and dirtiest man in pro football?" "Guilty," I said, smiling. Hey, why not? I just ran with it. By now it had taken on a life of its own.

(Incidentally, it was actually Dan and Jackie who cut off my pants' leg. All I can say is payback is a bitch, boys. The statute of limitations on these things can go on for decades, so watch out. I kept those one-legged pants and wrapped them up and gave them to Dan 10 years later when he retired from the NFL.)

The *Sports Illustrated* cover was a blessing and a curse for me. On one hand, it gave me recognition and fame that I had never comprehended prior to that, which was amazing. On the other hand, it limited my chances of getting any endorsement deals. Whereas a guy like Mean Joe Greene could endorse products, I was seen as too risky. Hell, I told my agent to at least try to get me a soap deal or something, where "dirty" could be spun as a good thing, but it never worked out. My reputation made me a liability. I did wind up becoming the spokesperson for Miller Lite beer years later, but that was based more on my image as a troublemaker and agitator. I also later did a Bic razor commercial with several tough guys, including Mean Joe Greene, Hacksaw Reynolds, and L.C. Greenwood, for their "toughest beards" campaign, which was also pretty neat.

After the *SI* cover, I was called everything in the book: cheap-shot art-ist, dirty, nasty, mean, villain, hitman, evil—you name it. I was the Snidely Whiplash of the NFL. Hell, I even had several credible death threats after that. No kidding, they had to assign security to me and everything. I felt like the freaking president out there, with Secret Service guys ready to take a bullet for me. That was something else.

Speaking of taking bullets, I also drew a lot of penalties for my team by having rival players cheap shot me. I earned my teams *a lot* of yardage over the years. Sure, I got my fair share of penalties too, but I got away with a lot more than I ever got caught for. To know where the refs are, and to know what you can and can't get away with, is a real art form. Frustrating and agitating was my gift. I was world-class at it. The bottom line was that my opponents hated me but my teammates loved me. One of the greatest compliments I ever got was from a little kid many years later who told me that he wanted to be an offensive lineman. Hell, that would have *never* happened in my day. No way. So I would like to think that I helped make it cool to be a lineman, which was all right by me.

As for the 1977 season, we wound up posting a pretty marginal 7–7 record and ultimately missed the playoffs. It was pretty disappointing to say the least. One of the highlights came in Week 7, when we blanked the Giants 28–0. I scored my first and only touchdown that night, and I did it while battling maybe the worst hangover of my life. Thank God it was a Monday night game too, because I was still throwing up all afternoon from being out at one of my old college teammate's weddings. That was a rough one.

Meanwhile, one of the lowlights of the season occurred on Thanks-giving Day in a game against the Dolphins in St. Louis. It was our third game in 10 days and we were spent. They were killing us 55–14 late in the game and their loud-mouthed rookie defensive end, A.J. Duhe, started talking shit to us on the line of scrimmage, telling us how much we sucked. So I went back to the huddle and said that we needed to take care of him. Sure enough, on the next play our center, Tom Banks, ran straight over and speared him in the throat. I saw him getting up and the whistle hadn't blown, so I figured I would get a piece of that sonofabitch, too. I wasn't about to take any shit from a snot-nosed, cocky rookie, so I went over and speared him in the chest for good measure.

Well, on the next play their two biggest linebackers, Bob Matheson and Kim Bokamper, lined up right across from me and proceeded to tell me that I was a dead man. They ignored the ball carrier and came right at me. I couldn't escape, so I grabbed both of their face masks and dragged them down to the ground with me. From there, we went at it and all hell broke loose. Fists were flying everywhere. Pretty soon fights broke out all over the field and both benches emptied. It was nuts. When the referee came over to eject me, he started shoving me toward the sideline. Instinctively, I shoved back and wound up accidentally knocking him right on his ass. Big mistake. The officials are untouchable, and I knew I was going to have my ass handed to me for that one.

Upset at what I had done, and about the ensuing fine and suspension I feared lie ahead, I took off my helmet and threw it as high into the air as I could. When it landed, it exploded all over the turf. Coryell and Hanifan tried to calm me down, but I was like a raging bull. Hanifan grabbed my arm, and when I pulled back I accidentally ripped the headset right off his head, nearly decapitating the poor guy. Luckily his toupee stayed put; it would have been a disaster if that thing flew off on live TV.

The next morning I wound up on the covers of nearly every newspaper in the country, alongside words like "dirty," "cheap-shotter," and "disgrace." When the dust settled I wound up being summoned to meet with NFL commissioner Pete Rozelle. It just so happened that our next game was against the Giants in New York, so the decision was made to just leave me there after our game to meet with him. Well, we wound up getting beat 27–7, and after the game I went out for drinks with a few of the Giants players to a joint called Tittle Tattle, a famous bar in Manhattan regularly frequented by the local sports celebrities. After several drinks, Giants guard John Hicks and his teammate Jack Gregory, a defensive end, got into a fight with one another. I think it was over a woman, I can't remember. They were really going at it though, knocking over tables and breaking glasses everywhere. It was crazy. I stayed the hell out of it, not wanting to get into any more trouble. Plus, I was chatting up a pretty young stewardess at the time and didn't want to be bothered.

I got back to my hotel at about 4:30 in the morning. Instead of going to bed I just showered, put on my suit, and walked down to the league offices to take my medicine. Once I got there I sat down in the lobby. Sitting there next to me was that morning's *New York Post*. To my horror, I looked at the headline on the cover of the sports page, which read: "Two Giants, Dobler in Barroom Fracas." I was so shocked that I literally spit my coffee all over the paper. Trouble just seemed to have a way of finding me. I was doomed.

I went in to meet with the commish and as expected, he read me the riot act. I pleaded with him that I was just trying to defend and protect my quarterback, but once again my reputation had preceded me. He then called in Art McNally, the league's head of officials, to really rough me up. The three of us then walked over to a private screening room to watch a specially prepared video highlight reel of yours truly. I felt like I was being led down death row. They turned it on and there I was in all my glory. Cheap shot after cheap shot was played from the past six years of my career. I didn't even remember half of the stuff. There were clips of me punching guys, hitting them out of bounds, chop blocking, leg whipping, stepping on face masks, kneeing, and my personal favorite, knocking them over the pile. Of course there was a good share of holding calls, too. I was busted. I kept my mouth shut and listened to them lecture me about how I needed to clean up my act or else I would be out of a job. I had officially been put on notice.

I rejoined my teammates the next day and was welcomed back like a warrior returning from battle. We had won six in a row midway through the year, but then we fell apart in the end and lost our last four games. We still had a shot to get into the playoffs though, if Washington lost and we could beat Tampa Bay in the last game. So we flew down there where they promptly beat us 17–7. We played like shit. After the game we all knew that our run together was over. Our owner, Bill Bidwell, even locked Coryell out of his office. It was ugly. Don still had two years left on his contract, but Bill wouldn't release him from it. He would have rather paid him to sit at home for two years than let him go to one of our competitors. So, Don quit. Bill was a real piece of work.

I remember being at the Pro Bowl in Tampa a few weeks later partly because it was the first time they allowed female reporters in the locker room. It started to rain, so we had to do the press conference in the locker rooms. The coaches told us to show a little respect to the women that were present. Well, we were beat and just wanted to get cleaned up and go out and have a few beers, but they took so long setting everything up that we just started getting naked and stuff. One guy just stood there with his dick hanging out and did the interview with a female reporter.

I was at that Pro Bowl when I heard that Don had been forced out, and I was upset. I was pretty full of myself in those days and enjoyed talking to the media. So when a reporter asked me what I thought about the situation, I arrogantly replied, "Hey, if a successful coach like Don can get fired, then I suppose a Pro Bowler like me could get traded, too." I was basically saying that nobody on our roster was safe. Well, the headline in the paper the next day read "Dobler Asks to Be Traded." Ah, the media…

When our general manager, Joe Sullivan, read that story, he was pissed. When a reporter asked him about my quote, he said, "If Dobler wants to get traded, we can certainly accommodate him." The guy wasn't fucking around either, because the very next day he dealt me to New Orleans. I heard the news while I was still up at the Pro Bowl. To say I was shocked would be an understatement. I just tried to stay positive. As one writer put it, in a Biblical sense I was being elevated from Cardinal to Saint.

As soon as I got back, however, the reality set in that my days as a Cardinal were officially over. Sure, I was sad to be leaving my teammates in St. Louis, but this was a new opportunity. I was ready for a change, too. It was a turbulent time for us, the three musketeers: Dan and Tommy and me. Tommy had some demons and was mixed up in drugs, and Dierdorf had other aspirations beyond football that were taking shape. He had been going through a divorce and was running around with a lot of big-time movers and shakers. His days of going out and drinking and carousing and being rowdy with me and the guys were over by then, so the time was right for me to move on. He invested his money wisely into a lot of local business deals, such as a pool company, and he was really a part of the St. Louis society. He had endorsement deals and was very well known around town. Dan was very politically correct and honorable in everything he did. Everybody loved him and he never got in trouble. Nobody had any dirt on him, and he was so well respected that even if they had any, they wouldn't expose it because they liked him too much. He was, and is, a great guy. He is like a brother to me; I love the guy.

When I found out how much the Saints were going to pay me, I nearly pissed myself. I signed a $125,000 contract, including a fat $60,000 bonus, which was more than my entire base salary in St. Louis at the time. I couldn't believe it. Just to rub it in, I even gave a quote to a reporter about how crazy it was that an offensive lineman was now making more than Jim Hart, the starting quarterback in St. Louis. It was a direct shot at Bill Bidwell, who was notoriously cheap. I just wanted to stir it up and cause a little turmoil, which I did. I was a little bitter about being dealt the way that I was, so I felt entitled to give a little parting shot.

I also used the opportunity of moving and starting over to get my shit together with Linda. I was nervous about being with a new team, so instinctively I came back to her. She was my security blanket. Sure, I had fooled around that season and gotten some things out of my system. But I was ready to settle down again. We had stayed in touch that year, and I would travel to Laramie on my days off to be with her and Mark. It wasn't like I had totally written her off. I would call every night to say hi and to talk to Mark, and they even came down for a few games. Anyway, I called her and we talked and she agreed that we should get our family back together at that point. From there we bought a new house down in New Orleans. I was happy as hell that she was as understanding as she was and that she wanted to start over again after a six-month hiatus.

She took me back with open arms and I was extremely lucky that she let me do what I did. I really appreciated it. It certainly wasn't normal by anybody else's standards, but it worked for us and that was all that mattered. I didn't want to rationalize what I had done, and I certainly didn't want to discuss it. I just wanted to move past it and get on with my life. I have never been a touchy-feely guy who enjoys sharing his deepest feelings. If I could get away with not having to discuss it, that was fine with me. Needless to say, a change of scenery was going to be just what the doctor ordered. In the end, being traded to New Orleans saved my marriage...at least for the time being.

4

FROM THE BIG EASY TO BUFFALO

*"The process I had to go through
just to get ready for games was amazing.
The icing, the deicing, the taping, the braces,
the stretching, the painkillers—
it was an adventure just getting my body
to the point where I could suit up and play."*

I began the 1978 season as a member of the New Orleans Saints. I remember being introduced to the media at a news conference at the famous Pat O'Brien's bar down in the French Quarter along Bourbon Street. Saints head coach Dick Nolan was there, and I was excited to be playing for a team that had traded for me. It was nice to be wanted. As a player, I was excited to learn a new system under a new coaching staff. I came into training camp and was anxious to fit in. I was in great shape, too. I remember running the mile-and-a-half in just over nine minutes, which was pretty damn good for a 275-pound lineman. The Saints were a decent team. Archie Manning was the quarterback and there were some solid players on the roster. My reputation had preceded me, and I could tell that while some of the players were thrilled to have me on their team, a handful of others were either scared or jealous of me. So I knew that I was going to have to earn their respect. I worked hard coming into training camp and was determined to lead by example.

Everything was going fine until I got my finger tangled up in a guy's jersey during the first day of camp. It got busted up pretty badly and as a result I had to have surgery to get a pin put in it. I was so pissed. I wound up missing the entire training camp. I was determined not to miss any games though, so I had the doctors put a huge cast on my entire hand and forearm that would allow me to play. We wrapped it in tape and then foam, and it looked enormous. It added about four inches to my reach, which was awesome. I could stick that in my opponent's neck, chest, or face, and he couldn't reach me to get back. Or if a guy tried to bull rush past me, I would catch that sonofabitch right on the chin with an upper-cut. *Wham.* Needless to say, that cast was a wonderful new addition to my bag of tricks. Now, was that "dirty"? I would say it was resourceful. But hey, that's just me.

We opened the season with a 31–24 win over the Vikings at home in the Superdome but then lost to Green Bay in Week 2. I was playing well and was gelling with my new linemates. Our next game, against the Eagles, was where things started to go south for me in a hurry. I got tied up on a play midway through the game and was injured pretty badly. I got taped up and tried to keep playing but I could hardly run. A few plays later I got hung up again, and this time I wound up tearing a ligament in my knee. They had to haul me off on a cart and I was out for the rest of the season. It was brutal. Ironically, the guy I got hung up on was Pro Bowl linebacker Bill Bergey, who I had taken out the previous season in St. Louis during the third game of the year. Neither incident was inten-tional, but like I have always said, karma is a bitch.

It wasn't my first run-in with Bill either. We had a tussle a few years earlier during a game in St. Louis. I remember we were beating them pretty good with just a few seconds left in the game. We were down on their 1-yard line and they were expecting us to just take a knee. Well, for some reason Hart handed the ball off to Terry Metcalf and he walked in for a touchdown. The Eagles players were pissed. Bergey was especially upset and started mouthing off to me about how we were trying to show them up. I didn't want to get into it with him, so I just turned and headed for the locker room. I wasn't on the extra-point team, so I figured that as long as the game was over I was going to hit the showers. We had won and my day was over.

Well, as I was walking past Bergey to get to the tunnel, he got up in my face. So I slapped him upside the head, and the next thing I knew he jumped on my back. We started going at it and sure enough, the officials threw us both out of the game. I started pleading with the ref to just let me go. I said, "Wait a minute, I was leaving. I didn't do a thing. He attacked me." Well, the ref didn't care. He ejected us both and we each got a $250 fine. It was the most expensive shower I ever took. Afterward, we were both mingling around this lobby area near the locker rooms and I went over to him. I smiled at him and said, "Are we two of the stupidest sons of bitches in the world or what? We might be the only players in the history of the league to get thrown out of a game after it was already over." We both just laughed it off.

Not being able to play for the rest of my first season with the Saints was really tough. I had never had to sit out like that before. I actually sat in the stands with my family instead of sitting on the bench, which was odd, but that was where they wanted me. I continued to work hard though. I would come in at 5:30 in the morning to get treatment on my knee. I tried my best to avoid seeing the other players. When you're injured, you are like the walking dead. No one wants to communicate with you or hang out with you because they are afraid the injury "juju" will rub off on them. It sounds crazy, but we are a pretty superstitious bunch, us football players. I was also sort of self-conscious about how the other players felt about me sitting out. The organization had traded two pretty good players to get me and they were paying me handsomely, and here I was sitting in the stands during our games. I am no economist, but I am sure that was not the return on investment they were hoping for.

I just tried to stay sane. I lived in a subdivision with several other players, so it was fun to be able to socialize with them and their families. We would go out for dinner with other couples on Friday nights. Linda and I had a pretty normal life there. We would take Mark to the zoo and to movies and have family dinners. It was a nice time. I hate to say it, but we were like Ozzie and Harriet. I think because we didn't know a lot of people the way we had in St. Louis, we clung to each other pretty tightly. The "Big Easy" was a great place with a ton of fun stuff to do. As a result, a lot of our friends and family came down to visit us. That was just what we needed at that time in our lives.

Another neat thing that I remember was being able to take Mark down into the locker room with me after games. He would help me take my pads off and that kind of stuff, which was pretty great. He got to know a lot of the other players' kids on Saturday afternoon walkthroughs too, including the Manning boys, Peyton and Eli, who were always running around out there on the Astroturf. I could tell even back then that those kids had a real passion for football. It is amazing to think how far they have come, both being Super Bowl MVPs and multimillionaires. Incredible.

After a while the coaches wanted me to sit in on meetings and watch film. That was tough, to watch film knowing full well that I couldn't play on Sundays. I was bored, but I hung in there and tried to support my teammates. In retrospect, I should have ingratiated myself to the coaches and offered to work with the other linemen on their technique and on breaking down film. Who knows? Had I done that I might have gotten into coaching and had a completely different career path after my playing career was over. Looking back I regret not contributing more than I did. Of course the Cardinals' general manager, Joe Sullivan, said the reason they traded me was because they knew my knees were shot. Today the Cardinals are denying that my knees were ever bad in St. Louis.

In the end we wound up with a 7–9 record, which was the best record New Orleans had ever achieved. That off-season I commuted back and forth to Laramie. I would fly to Wyoming on Wednesday night and then come back to New Orleans for treatment with the trainers on Sunday. I would then fly back to Wyoming on Wednesday and do it all over again. It was tough. I did this on my own dime too, to prove to the coaches that I was serious about rehabbing. Not only did I want to make sure that the coaches knew I was working hard, I also wanted to make sure that they couldn't cut me for violating the terms of my contract by not doing everything necessary to get healthy. I was skeptical of the system and knew that other guys had been essentially fired for being injured, and I wanted to make sure that I wasn't one of them. I was scared. I knew that there was no pension or disability plan for us, so I made sure that I was extremely visible. I figured that there was no way a lawyer could say that I wasn't working hard on my treatment. No way.

During that time, I stayed focused on my rehab and out of trouble. When I was in New Orleans by myself for a few nights a week, I didn't go out drinking and I didn't chase women. I was done with that. Linda had given me her trust and I didn't want to mess that up. Looking back, it was probably the most normal, relaxed time in my life. I had that perfect balance of family time and personal time for myself. I also got involved with the media, which was neat. In addition to co-hosting a radio show a couple nights a week, I even got to fill in as the sports anchor for one of the local TV news affiliates one night a week. I was pretty good at it, despite the fact that some of those goddamn Cajun names were pretty tough to pronounce.

I came into training camp reinvigorated. My knee was still pretty bad, but I made the best of it. I had torn the cruciate ligament, which allows you to move forward and backward, and they tried to make a new one for me but it never took. They didn't have arthroscopic surgery or anything like that in those days; they just sliced you open and cut out the cartilage. It was just bone on bone at that point. As one player put it, my scarred knees "looked like they lost a knife fight with a midget." I never made a fuss over it though, because the last thing I wanted to do was draw attention to myself. I just shut up and played football. I had become a smarter, more efficient player and learned to do more with less. I was more comfortable in my own skin. I had learned some tricks along the way and was now able to put them to good use.

I was able to really work with my offensive linemates during training camp, to get us all on the same page. It would pay off for us, too. We wound up going 8–8 in 1979, the best the franchise had ever done, and we damn near made the playoffs. I remember sitting down with quarter-back Archie Manning one day to talk to him about how offensive linemen just hate to give up sacks. I told him that when we gave up a sack, it killed our confidence because the whole world knew that we just got beat. I told him that I could block my guy all day long and no one would ever say I was a great blocker. But if my guy beat me just one time, then he could wind up being the hero of the game. It's like that old saying, "You suck one cock, and you're a cocksucker for life."

Well, I didn't want to be a cocksucker, which meant I wanted Archie to get rid of the football if nobody was open rather than taking a sack. I told him that I wanted to lead the NFL in the least number of sacks allowed and that I needed his help to do it. It was a two-way street; we protected him, and sometimes he had to protect us. Archie took 36 sacks the year before I got there and was notorious for being an immobile, flat-footed statue that would collapse in the pocket. Well, sure enough, he bought into what I was saying and we wound up allowing only 17 sacks. That meant a great deal to me. The Saints had never led the league in that stat before and I think the nastiness I brought to the team gave us a big boost.

After the season I continued to train hard, flying back and forth from New Orleans to Wyoming at my own expense. I got my treatment and was doing everything I could to stay healthy. My leg was still gimpy but I knew that I had just anchored one of the top offensive lines in the league, so I felt good about the upcoming 1980 season. We had a good young team and I was excited to get back out there. Then, out of the blue, Saints head coach Dick Nolan called me and told me that I had been traded to Buffalo. I was speechless. Then I got pissed. I knew that my knee had scared the hell out of them and that they figured I was going to be a liability. They got nothing more than a conditional draft pick for me, which totally bummed me out. I got this call two days before I was to go to training camp with the Saints. There were a lot of questions. What about my house in New Orleans? What about the car we left there? What about the furniture? It was a very stressful two days. At least I already had a lot of winter clothes.

Maybe it was my public image that had become a liability. One of the things that always made me feel somewhat uncomfortable was the fact that during the pregame introductions, they would play "When the Saints Come Marching In" for all the players but then played "Macho Man" for me. The fans thought it was cute, but it might have rubbed a few people in high places the wrong way. Who knows? Either way, I was done in Louisiana and was going to have to reinvent myself yet again in upstate New York. Hell, I didn't even know where Buffalo was. If you ask the average guy how many professional teams the state of New York has, he will tell you two: the Giants and the Jets. People always forget about the Buffalo Bills.

With that, I packed up and headed up to Buffalo to get situated. Chuck Knox, who had great success leading the Rams throughout the 1970s, was the Bills' head coach and I had a lot of respect for him. I knew him from my Pro Bowl days; he was the coach of the NFC team for all three years that I played in it. He traded for me too, and it was nice to again be going somewhere I was wanted. Their training camp started in just a few days and I didn't have a lot of time to mess around. When I got there the first thing I did was look at a schedule. To my utter delight, guess who their third opponent was that year? The Saints, in New Orleans. I had my motivation: I was going to stick it to that sonofabitch Dick Nolan for trading me.

I made it through camp but not without dealing with a little bit of turmoil along the way. The Bills' starting guard, future Hall of Famer Joe DeLamielleure, wasn't happy being there and they were trying to negotiate a new contract with him. I later found out that I was brought in for two reasons: first, to force his hand and serve as leverage, which sucked for me; and second, to take his place on the roster if he did indeed leave. It was a little bit humbling coming in under those conditions. It was like my freshman year in college when I found out that there were 115 other full-ride scholarships given out. I wasn't all that important. Well, Joe ultimately wound up signing with Cleveland but not before causing a whole bunch of drama. In fact, I got put on waivers just 24 hours before our first game. They figured nobody would claim me, so they threw me out there. I was pissed about that, but I realized that it was a business decision, not a personal one. Hell, I was 30 years old by then and barely had one good leg to stand on. I was a piece of meat in their eyes. Luckily it worked out in the end because I got through waivers and was able to stay put. Once DeLamielleure left, I was inserted as the starting right guard. If he had chosen to re-sign, I probably would have been cut the day before the start of the regular season. I would have been completely screwed as far as making another roster at that point. It was just like my rookie year all over again.

One of the things that really pissed me off about being put on waivers, however, was that I had to sign a new contract all over again. In fact, they actually brought it to me the morning of our first game. I was certainly no agent, but I looked it over and it seemed okay. The money was the same, which was what I cared about the most, so I signed it. What I didn't realize at the time was that they had crossed out my rights to workman's compensation and disability insurance. I never initialed that part or anything. They just went and did it. I didn't notice it and it never became an issue until years and years later, when I started having some serious medical problems. I went to the union to apply for workman's compensation and it was denied. That contract was altered back in 1980 and believe it or not, I am still working on resolving this issue almost 30 years later. Unbelievable.

Anyway, we had a really good, young team and wound up beating Miami in the opener. Buffalo hadn't beaten the Dolphins in our last 20 meetings, spanning an entire decade, so our fans went nuts. They stormed the field and even tore down the goal posts, which was pretty crazy. I could tell right away that the fans up there were really intense. They love their Bills. After beating the Jets in Week 2 we headed down to

New Orleans to do battle with the Saints. I remember running out onto the field and giving Nolan the "Italian salute." I was really pumped up. We kicked their ass 35–26 and I played great. It was extremely satisfying to play well and to stick it to them. They totally fell apart that year and went 1–15. In fact, that was the year that they became known as the "Aints," and their fans were coming to games wearing paper bags over their heads.

In retrospect, it was a blessing in disguise to get out of New Orleans when I did. I sometimes wonder if the Saints' season would have tanked like that if I had remained with them. Who knows if I was that good? I like to think I made a difference, so maybe things would have been different.

In Buffalo, we won our first five games that season, and we were having a lot of fun. My best friend on the team was former Raiders linebacker Phil Villapiano. We had battled against each other in years past, but now we were roommates and partners in crime. He was just as crazy as I was and we hit it off right away. Whereas the bars in most cities closed at 1:00 in the morning, in Buffalo they didn't shut down until 4:00. Needless to say, we did our fair share of late-night partying together. Phil and I would use our own brand of motivation to rally the troops. He would throw chairs in team meetings and I placed bounties on opposing players' heads. Together we made a lot of noise. We would say some pretty outlandish stuff too, like "Let's go out there and rip their heads off and shit down their necks." It was all for show, but the other guys would get fired up. It was fun. My entire attitude had changed that season. I had a new role: to get my teammates fired up. Hell, I even wore No. 69 on my jersey. Tell me *that* wasn't a statement. It was good for starting conversations with the ladies, that was for sure.

Phil and I were both older veterans and we figured they had brought us in to teach the younger guys how to be a "pro's pro." We also had to clean up a lot of their messes, too. Knox used to lean on us to handle any locker room disputes or fracases that would erupt. That was our role and we did it. Hell, we were both just happy to have jobs at that point. Phil and I are still great friends to this day. I remember one time when we were on a flight home from playing out on the West Coast and a fight broke out between two players. Chuck just looked at Phil and I and said, "Go clean that up." We went back there and broke it up; that way when the press asked Chuck about what happened, he could deny knowing anything about it.

I remember another time when there was a member of the press, a young kid, hanging out with some of the players in the back of the plane. I saw this and went back to tell him to please go back to the front with the other members of the media. He smiled and said, "No, it's cool. I'm all right." Well, there were players in the bathrooms snorting all sorts of things up their noses, and he certainly didn't need to see that. I didn't want that fact getting out and causing a distraction. I learned a long time ago there was nothing that was truly "off the record." So, after politely asking this kid to go back to his seat, I grabbed him by his neck and threatened to carry him there by his head. He took off at that point like a scared bunny. Mission accomplished.

Chuck knew that my knees were shot and he would let me slide during running drills and stuff like that so I wouldn't wear out. He cut me some slack and I really appreciated that. He knew that there were only so many miles left on my tires. Playing up there in the winter really made it tough on my body. We didn't have an indoor training facility in those days and had to practice outside every day. That was so hard on my knees, to be on the ice and snow every day. I had severe arthritis and that cold weather made it ache, night and day. By now I was dragging my back foot when I would pull on certain plays, too. I couldn't hide it anymore; I was still effective as a guard, but I was slowing down. Looking back, I couldn't believe how proficient I actually was, considering how messed up my knees were. As dumb as I was, I had actually become a pretty smart player.

My list of injuries at that point was really unbelievable. The process I had to go through just to get ready for games was amazing. The icing, the deicing, the taping, the braces, the stretching, the painkillers—it was an adventure just getting my body to the point where I could suit up and play. I would get to games several hours early to sit in a series of warm and cold whirlpools. I would then get a massage, followed by more heat and cold. Then I would go through my taping ritual, which could take an hour by itself. Each finger, every joint. That was my thing. Talk about high maintenance. After games I could barely get into the shower. My leg would stiffen up and I simply couldn't bend it. Hell, the next day it would take all of my strength just to get out of bed. I was a mess.

Playing hurt was just something we did in those days, no matter what. We were always told, "You can't make the club in the tub," so we just shut our mouths and played football. If you were in pain, you played. Period. I remember one game my shoulder was so messed up I literally couldn't move it. It was all busted and dislocated, but there was no way in hell I was coming out. I was pass protecting with one arm, praying that I wouldn't get beat so that the coaches would be on to me. I knew that if I came out of the game that another guy would be there to take my spot, so I played through it. That was my mentality. Hell, that was everybody's mentality in those days.

Playing hurt went a long way toward earning the respect of your teammates, too. Sometimes when I played, I was so beat up I could barely get around. But when my teammates saw me go out there and compete better than a lot of healthy players, they got motivated themselves. A lot of guys even told me that I was an inspiration to them, which meant a great deal to me. A lot of the players today don't know the difference between pain and injury. Shit, football is a collision sport, and playing hurt is just a part of it. Pain is not injury. Pain is something you have to overcome and play through. They don't do that today. Their agents tell them that if they play hurt then they will shorten their careers. It was a totally different era back in my day. We weren't given the option of sitting out if we were experiencing a little discomfort or pain.

We eventually finished the year with a pretty damn good 11–5 record and won the AFC Eastern Division. I remember beating San Francisco in the regular-season finale 18–13 out in their muddy and sloppy field. From there, instead of heading back to Buffalo, we flew down to Vero Beach, Florida, to prepare for the playoffs in the warm weather. What a treat that was. Our wives were so jealous. The great thing about Vero was that I knew it like the back of my hand. Vero was where the Saints used to have their training camp, so I knew where all the good bars were. Phil and I were out of control down there. I remember Knox saying, "You know, if you and Phil would spend as much time studying your game plan and working to be better football players as you did partying all of the time, you would both be Hall of Famers." He was probably right.

After several days in Vero we then headed over to San Diego to play the Chargers in the opening round of the playoffs. After spending a week in the sun we all felt rejuvenated…maybe even a little too rejuvenated. We jumped out to an early 14–3 lead and thought that we had it in the bag. That's when their All-Pro quarterback, Dan Fouts, got hot and led a late rally. They wound up winning the game 20–14, thus ending our season. We were all pretty devastated. It was a long flight home.

One bright spot for me, however, was the fact that our offensive line led the league in fewest number of sacks allowed. I remember talking to our quarterback, Joe Ferguson, and telling him the same thing I had told Archie Manning the year before—get rid of the ball if it looks like you are going to get sacked. He wasn't the most mobile guy either, so he took the advice and sure enough it made a big difference. I remember toward the end of the season, we had given up just five sacks all year. Then Ferguson sprained his ankle and his backup, Dan Manucci, came in. Well, he wasn't very prepared and certainly didn't have the common sense that Joe did because he got sacked eight times against New England. Eight! And we still wound up leading the league. Man, we were pissed though. We had worked so hard to break the record and we were on pace to do it. Then Manucci comes in and it was all over in a heartbeat. Our entire offensive line went to Coach Knox after the game and told him that we would rather play with Joe Ferguson in a goddamn cast or David Humm than with Dan Manucci.

Buffalo had a long history of good offensive lines and it was neat to be able to restore that tradition. They had been struggling for a couple of years after the guys who blocked for Hall of Fame running back O.J. Simpson (known as "the Electric Company" because they "turned on the Juice") had left. For those guys, it was all about getting O.J. into the Pro Bowl. Well, not only did we lead the league in fewest sacks, we also had a Pro Bowl running back of our own in Joe Cribbs. I would say we did a pretty damn good job.

Every team I played for—St. Louis, New Orleans, and then Buffalo—led the league in fewest sacks allowed as soon as I came in. None of them led the league before I got there and they didn't lead the league after I left. So it was no fluke. I certainly didn't do it by myself, but I think I was a pretty good influence. I think I brought a blend of mental and physical toughness. I got the offensive line to come together as a group, to become one. It was us against them; we hated defenses. They were the donkeys in our eyes. We took pride in what we did and we stuck together. I hope that is a part of my legacy. To quote Walt Disney, "It seems to me shallow and arrogant for any man in these times to claim he is completely self-made, that he owes all of his success to his own unaided efforts. Many hands and hearts and minds generally contribute to anyone's notable achievements."

After the season Linda and I packed up and moved back to Wyoming. We had been renting a place in Buffalo and were anxious to be going home. When I got home I was spending some time with a buddy of mine who was a real estate broker. Well, one thing led to another and I wound up buying a 1,000-acre ranch about a mile outside of Laramie. To this day, I don't know why in the hell I did it. Interest rates were around 17 percent at the time and I had no business buying a ranch. None. But I thought I was a big shot and figured that was what big shots did. I got completely overextended financially and it turned out to be a disaster. I thought I would become a gentleman rancher, but I found out that there was a lot of work to be done on a working ranch, and it ended up being a huge money pit.

The one good thing about the ranch was the enormous barn that we used to throw some great parties. I would get together with 10 of my business associates and we would each put in $500. We would then each invite 50 couples and have one hell of a party. We would hire a band and get catered barbeque; it was amazing. With 500 people you could imagine things would get out of hand sometimes, too.

Sadly, I had fallen back into some of my destructive ways and was once again out of control. I remember going outside for some air one night during one of our parties and getting a little action from this gal I had just met. I didn't think anything of it. We stepped into this tool shed and started going at it. She was going down on me and then all of a sudden she said that her legs were getting tired. Well, I didn't want her to stop, so I grabbed this milk crate that was full of brand-new, really expensive power tools and just dumped everything out on the floor. *Crash*. I had that crate set up for her to sit down comfortably on in about one-tenth of a second. It was as quick as a NASCAR pit stop. God, I can't believe my poor wife had to put up with me. She was pregnant with our first child together at the time, too. Hey, I am not proud of what I did. But I did it.

We headed back to Buffalo that summer for training camp. Linda was going to be delivering the baby at any moment and it was pretty stressful. I remember going to Coach Knox to tell him I was going to be taking a few days off for the birth. We were going to be inducing, and it was important for me to be there. Well, Chuck thought that I was asking for his permission and gave me the old "You gotta do what you think is right, Conrad" speech. He didn't say yes and he didn't say no, which I thought was pretty shitty. The reality was that I wasn't asking him, I was telling him. He didn't appreciate that, but I figured as a 10-year veteran I had earned that right. Sure enough, our beautiful daughter Erin was born on August 1, 1981, and I was very happy. We had a baptism shortly thereafter and Phil, who was Erin's godfather, insisted on throwing a big party for all the guys on the team.

Back at training camp I was excited to see all the guys again and to blow off some steam. My ranch had drained me financially and my knees were hurting. I needed to get back out onto the football field to relieve some of my aggression. I was pretty nervous though. I knew that my knees were barely allowing me to do my job at that point. I was really in a lot of pain but I needed to keep playing. Things were different now; I needed the money. After all, I had mortgages to pay and mouths to feed.

The Bills had drafted guard Jim Ritcher in the first round the year before. He was a huge kid from North Carolina State and had just won the coveted Outland Trophy, given to the nation's top lineman. The guy was really good and would go on to play in the NFL for 16 years. Anyway, he was my heir apparent; the writing was now on the wall and I was feeling the pressure, big time.

I knew that if I made any mistakes that season, I would get benched and become a backup. While some guys relished the thought of being a backup, it did nothing for me. I wanted to play. Beyond that, I knew that if I wasn't starting I probably wouldn't be able to play at all. My knees were so shot that I couldn't stand around for long periods of time, so I would get treatment on them before the game started right up until the National Anthem. I would then run out there all ready to go. If I had to sit on the bench, they would stiffen up and I wouldn't be able to walk. I had to go from the training room directly to the field to do battle—no detours.

All that treatment, along with a handful of amphetamines, and I was good to go. Hey, I did what I had to do. Many of us did. Shit, I would say at least half of the guys from my era took "bennies" before games. They took the edge off. They were amazing, because despite the fact that I literally couldn't walk on Mondays and Tuesdays, on game days I could do a full split. I am sure my adrenaline was pumping too, but the drugs gave you energy and helped blocked out the pain. Truth be told, I don't think I could have played at that stage of my career without them. Sometimes they would make you a little bit crazy, too. Looking back, I was out of control those last two years in Buffalo. I was on a lot of "medication" in those days. I was hurting and had to get up for the games. I used to smoke cigarettes before games, and I would even have a few at halftime. I was like a wild dog at times. I was a mess.

I also did something stupid that season that I still feel bad about to this day: I caved in to peer pressure and deliberately tried to hurt a guy, all for the entertainment of my teammates. We were playing Baltimore and during a players-only meeting Phil got up in front of the entire team and begged me to make a vow that Colts defensive end Mike Barnes wouldn't finish the game. I said no way, that I didn't do stuff like that. Phil then started to egg me on, getting the entire team to chant "Vow, Conrad! Vow, Conrad!" It was immature, unnecessary, and stupid, but I wanted to do whatever I could to motivate the guys. I knew that I was on the edge of being irrelevant, so I caved in. I got up very slowly and quietly said, "The motherfucker won't finish…" The room erupted before I could even finish the sentence. Guys started throwing chairs and desks, and somebody even smashed the chalkboard. It was insane.

Once the game started, I went right after Barnes. I leg whipped him every chance I got and really let him have it. My ankles and knees were throbbing from hitting him so hard, but I wanted to keep my vow. Eventually he hobbled off the field with a hyperextended knee. It was the most unsatisfying thing I had ever done. Amidst the cheers of my teammates, I knew that I had sunk to a new low. After the game I told Phil to never do that again. I was ashamed of myself.

Another bizarre moment from that season happened a few weeks later during a Monday night game against Dallas. I had leg whipped my opponent, John Dutton, and had gotten a couple of personal foul penalties. I then got a holding call shortly thereafter. Coach Knox was pissed, so he sent in Jim Richter to replace me. Once Jim got into the huddle, I refused to come out and sent him back to the sideline. So Knox sent him in again, and I sent him back out again. Each time he came in, I refused to leave and just kept sending Jim back to the sideline. We eventually punted and that was when I finally came off the field. When I got to the sideline, I lost it and just started screaming at Chuck: "How dare you take a gladiator out of the arena! I am a fucking warrior! Are you fucking crazy?"

Chuck immediately turned to Phil and said, "Get this guy away from me." Phil then came running over and grabbed me before I did something really stupid. I wound up getting thrown out of the game, and the next day I had to go meet with Chuck in his office. He was really pissed at me for embarrassing him the way that I did. I tried to tell him that I was just trying to fire up the other players, but he could see through my bullshit. He decided to bench me for the following game against the Cardinals in St. Louis. It sucked, but I definitely deserved it.

Going back to St. Louis was pretty nostalgic. I actually had a pretty good time there too, despite the fact that I couldn't play. When we got there I wound up going out to dinner with Jim Hanifan—who was now the team's head coach—and Dan Dierdorf. They took me to this place across the border in Illinois so that nobody would see us. We even went in through the side door and sat in the back room, out of sight. It was like we were in the witness protection program or something. Here I was, having dinner with the coach and the captain of the opposing team.

The next day Dan and I had a chuckle about it out at midfield. You see, my teammates had voted me as team captain for the game, sort of thumbing their noses at Chuck for benching me at my homecoming. As a result, I got to go out and make the call for the coin flip before the game. We lost the flip and we lost the game 24–0. Riding the pines was tough. I desperately wanted to go in to play. Even though I knew I would be stiff as hell, I wanted to get in there so badly. Jim Ritcher was having a terrible game too, giving up sacks left and right, but Chuck's ego wouldn't let him put me in. I saw him looking at me several times, questioning whether or not to put me in, but he stayed true to his convictions. I sort of pouted on the sideline, but I respected his decision. He was the coach and he got paid to make those tough decisions, even if they weren't very popular. I came to realize at that point that when Chuck Knox told us how important it was to put aside our feelings for the success of the team, he was just blowing smoke. As I said before, pride is hard to swallow but it will go down. The coach put his decision above the good of the team. Right or wrong, I don't have an answer. But I do like to win, and I know if I was the coach, I would have swallowed my pride and put the best players on the field.

All in all, it was a good year. We played well down the stretch, winning four of our last five games to finish with a 10–6 record. Our regular-season finale was against the rival Dolphins in Miami. We wound up losing the game and I ended up getting into some more trouble to boot. Late in the game I got a holding penalty called on me that negated a key first down. I was blocking my guy and he bullrushed me right onto my back. I fell straight backward and the guy rushing me stepped right on my stomach and then fell on his ass. The referee then came over and called me for holding. I was so goddamned pissed. There were plenty of times in my career when I was guilty of holding, but this certainly wasn't one of them. I got beat and the guy bowled me over. I didn't even touch him. Afterward in the locker room I was really upset. The press came over to talk to me and I totally went off. I started cussing the referee out and calling him every name in the book. I told them that a bogus call like that could cost me my livelihood. I explained that if I lost my job then I would lose my house and I wouldn't be able to send my kids to college, yadda yadda yadda. I really went on a tirade.

I then said that I hoped the official who penalized me, John Keck, had something horrible happen to him in his lifetime that would directly affect his family so he would know how it felt. By now I was really on a roll and the media was eating it up. At that point I had an epiphany and realized that the next day's paper was probably going to read, "Conrad Dobler Wishes Harm on Official's Family." So I panicked and started going around the locker room, grabbing all of the reporter's notebooks, ripping them out of their hands and tearing pages out. Some of the guys saw me coming and just ran out of the room. I had officially lost it. Phil then came over and tried to prevent me from doing any more damage to myself.

Well, the next day I had to call my old buddy Commissioner Rozelle and apologize not only to him, but also to the official. Luckily the official forgave me and I didn't get fined. In reality, he probably watched the tape of the play and realized what a horrible call he had made. Regardless, Coach Knox had no choice but to suspend me for the next week, a playoff game against the Jets at Shea Stadium in New York. Oh, I was mad. I wound up playing cheerleader again and luckily we came out on top 31–27. I remember Joe Ferguson had a pretty good game and our wide receiver, Frank Lewis, had more than 150 yards receiving to go along with a pair of touchdowns. It was the first playoff game I had ever won and I was pretty excited about it. I was one step closer to playing in a Super Bowl. I desperately wanted a ring because I knew that I was living on borrowed time. Beyond that, we got additional cash bonuses for each postseason victory, and quite frankly I wanted to get paid.

From there we headed to Cincinnati to face the Bengals in the next round. Our line was playing really well and our running back, Joe Cribbs, rushed for nearly 100 yards and two touchdowns. It was a really close game and we were in it right until the end. We were tied 21–21 late in the fourth quarter and we could have won the game had we been able to manage the clock better. We wound up getting a costly delay-of-game penalty and it ultimately cost us the game. Five measly yards were the difference in us going for it or not going for it. As a result we had to punt instead of being able to run the clock out and then go for the field goal. Bengals quarterback Kenny Anderson then iced it when he hit Cris Collinsworth on what turned out to be a 16-yard game-winning touchdown. I was crushed.

I don't know why, but I just knew that was going to be the last time I would ever set foot on a football field as a player. Sadly, I was right. I would find out later that my career was indeed over. It was tough. After the game I went around and shook everybody's hand. No regrets. No tears. Just good, heartfelt good-byes. I remember thinking long and hard about what I was going to do with the rest of my life on that plane ride back to Buffalo. I was 31 years old at the time and I had my whole life ahead of me, but I was scared. One career was over and another one was about to begin. What that was, however, I had no idea. As far as my life after football was concerned, I had failed to follow my six "Ps": Proper Preparation Prevents Piss-Poor Performance.

A short while later I announced my retirement. I wasn't going to wait around for Chuck Knox to tell me that I wasn't going to be brought back. I always tried to be irreverent, so instead of having a big news conference I called a reporter friend of mine, Frank Luksa, who wrote for the *Dallas Times Herald* newspaper. He always wrote pretty nice articles about me, so I thought I would reward him with the scoop. I called him and let him break the story. I didn't really say it was final, I just said I was going to take a year off to get my health back. I said that I was "physically unable to play at this time, but that I hoped to be able to resume my career at a later date." I left the door open because I didn't want to give it up just yet. In my mind I knew it was over, but I couldn't bring myself to say it. Anyway, Chuck was pissed that I didn't give the story to the Bills' beat writer, but I didn't care. I was pissed. I knew that they weren't going to bring me back so I wanted to go out on my own terms.

I almost made a comeback a few months later when I got a call from my old offensive line coach at Wyoming, Bill Baker. Bill was by then the director of player personnel for the Arizona Wranglers of the upstart United States Football League, and he wanted to know if I was interested in suiting up again. The USFL was a legitimate rival to the NFL and they had a lot of cash, but they needed some marquee names to draw in the fans. I told him I was interested, but that the $50,000 salary he was offering me was way too low. I told him that it was going to take at least $150,000 to get me to even consider exposing my already badly beaten corpse to another year of torture. They balked, so I stayed retired. Incidentally, I got another call the following year, this time from the Washington Federals, who offered me $100,000 to play in their final seven games of the season. I said yes, but the Wranglers still apparently owned my rights from the year before and demanded a pair of first-round draft picks in return for my services. Washington said no thanks, and the whole thing fell apart. Safe to say, I was officially retired.

Looking back at my playing career, I can only be thankful that I got in 10 wonderful seasons. Millions of kids grow up dreaming of playing in the NFL, and I had made it. For the select few who get there, most only last a couple of years. I lasted a decade. It was a helluva ride, that was for sure. I made some great friends and have some priceless memories. I learned a great deal from all of my different coaches and coordinators over the years. Each had his own philosophies on how to get from point A to point B and each was unique. Eventually I was able to create my own style that was an amalgam of all of those different approaches to the game. Sadly, by the time I finally got it all figured out, I was too old and too beat up to play. There was a clear evolution to my career though: St. Louis was my adolescent years; New Orleans was my adult years; and Buffalo was my crotchety, pissed-off old-man years. Yup, it was hard to believe that at 31 years old I was over-the-hill. I still hadn't yet figured out what I wanted to be when I grew up.

5

THE POST-NFL GLADIATOR

*"I remember sitting around talking
to all of these former NFL players,
drinking beer, and talking
about my situation back home.
The guys were blown away.
They couldn't believe what I was up to,
and they were amazed at how I kept
all the plates spinning."*

It's safe to say I have had my share of ups and downs in my business career and my personal life, and I have learned some things about myself—and about human nature—in the process. I was really rolling high in the mid-1970s and early 1980s while I was still playing in the NFL. I had developed a real gladiator mentality about being a big, tough, NFL lineman. I felt like the football field was a real battlefield, and as gladiators, players deserved the spoils of war: money, drugs, fame, and women. I had totally bought into my own persona, and it was like a drug that had blinded me to reality. I never really worried about things because I figured that as a gladiator, I could always keep the plates spinning like those guys do in the circus. I thought that things would just always work out and that somehow I deserved that kind of life. Well, I learned that I could not keep all the plates spinning. Eventually, some of them would have to come crashing down.

In the 1970s, I was into all sorts of businesses and investments. I had the 1,000-acre ranch in Laramie, Wyoming, and I had also worked on a number of business projects and investments, including a 10-unit apartment complex, a bank, a subdivision in the Sierra Madres outside of Encampment, and some condominiums in Jackson Hole. I later opened a bar named Block 11 and worked on an FM radio-tower project. I was part-owner of a racquetball facility in Laramie. I had a construction company, office buildings, warehouses in Wyoming, oil-drilling rigs in Louisiana, and even a farm in Iowa. I had also got into doing some real estate development with my brother Clifford in California. I had become a jack of all trades, but I was a master of none.

In hindsight, I came to realize that in business, timing and perseverance can be very important, although perseverance can be a double-edged sword. Sometimes it is good to know when to admit defeat, and sometimes it pays to hang on until the bitter end and fight for the win. On the football field, I played every play expecting to win my individual battle, but if we lost the game I didn't whine about it. I wasn't one of the guys kicking or throwing things around in the locker room. That wasn't going to do any good. I would focus on the next game, the next battle, expecting to win it. Even when it was obvious that we were going to lose a game, I would always try to hurt my opponent on every play, so that maybe the next time we met he would be a little bit less effective, a little bit more cautious. Football is a game of 100 percent effort on every play. That effort is what counts. Effort and the will to win is what can make the difference. For some reason, I didn't carry that attitude into the business world. I wasted a lot of time and lost a lot of opportunities to strike it rich because I chose not to persevere, and I didn't stick with my investments long enough for them to pay off.

Such was the case with the construction permit I purchased from the government to build this huge FM antenna on top of Elk Mountain in 1974. Before we could start construction, my partner died suddenly from a brain tumor. I felt that I was not experienced enough to complete the construction project, so I sold the permit for what I had paid for it and walked away. Who knows? Had I just held that permit for a few more years, I probably would have made millions building the tower and selling or leasing it to cell phone providers starting to provide service in the mid-1980s! With the real estate project in California, my brother and I realized later that if we had just held on to the vacant lots, we could have made more money than we did selling them off. And in 1978, I lost out on another business venture because I decided not to persevere and took the easy way out. In that deal, I sold the contracts I had on three condominiums in Jackson Hole for a quick profit of about $32,000. Had I built and closed on those condos instead, they would have been worth about $2 million now!

At other times, my ego would get in the way of a business deal. In 1980, I got involved with starting a bank in Laramie along with some local investors. I felt insecure about being around them, and one time I made an ass of myself during a meeting. A couple of the people in the room said something that made me feel inferior, so I barked back. I went around the table and asked each person what they did for a living. After they had all answered, I said, "Any of us sitting here could be a professor, right?" They agreed. "Any of us could own a construction company, right?" Heads nodded. "Any of us could be a politician, right?" Again, everyone agreed. Then I arrogantly said, "Well, there is only one of us who could play in the National Football League. Me. And that is why I will always be one up on all of you." What kind of asshole would say something like that, other than me? I mean, who does that? Saying things without thinking about others is what I tend to do though, and that gets me in trouble. Needless to say, the bank project didn't last very long.

The thing is that I don't fight fair. When someone makes a rude comment to me, I don't dance around the tree. I go right for the trunk and cut it down. That is my nature, for better or for worse. In football, if somebody gave me a cheap shot, I was going to take them out at the knees. If they said something disrespectful to me, I immediately responded with the cruelest, ugliest thing I could possibly think of. Then it was over. A lot of my arguments started out as slap fights, only I turned them into knife fights. I don't know why I do that at times, but I do. I have been told many times that I say things out loud that other people only think about saying. Sometimes I wonder, *Is that so wrong?* I don't know. I guess that is why I am such a polarizing figure. People tend to either love me or hate me, with not many in between. But in either case, they always remember me; I do make an impression. Of course, on the football field, *all* my opponents hated me!

Anyway, after the 1981 season in Buffalo, I moved back to Laramie with Linda, Mark, and Erin, where I hoped to develop a successful business career. It didn't take me very long to realize that I couldn't afford to keep paying for the ranch, so I found a guy who was looking for a ranch and I wound up trading it to him for his house. I did the entire transaction myself, without a realtor, in two months. At the end of the day, I still lost a six-figure chunk of money on the deal, but at least I was out from underneath that mortgage. With that, we moved into our new house. It was no 1,000-acre ranch, but it was pretty nice. I still had the house in New Orleans at this point too, which was hemorrhaging money. Luckily, I was finally able to get rid of that the next year as well.

In 1982–83, Clifford and I got involved in developing a subdivision of modular homes in a mobile-home park in Laramie. Well, the whole thing fell apart, and it turned out to be a disaster. This time it was Clifford who would not persevere. When things got complicated, he and his financial backers pulled out and I was left holding the bag. I guess I can't blame them; they were used to doing business in California, which was a little different than doing business in Wyoming. But this was really one of my biggest lost opportunities. If I would have had the wherewithal to continue that project, I would have had a very nice income over the next 20 years, maybe $8,000 a month or so. But it just wasn't to be. It was, however, another learning experience: make sure your business partners— your teammates—also understand the value of perseverance.

I was trying to do whatever I could do to provide for my family, which grew again when my daughter Abbey was born on March 26, 1983. So I moved from one business venture to another whenever opportunities presented themselves. When the deal with Clifford fell apart, I started working with the guy we sold out to in Cheyenne doing real estate development. In 1984, I finally got some investors together, and we started our own subdivision in Greeley, Colorado. More plates spinning.

As if I did not have enough to do, I also got a gig working for an alcohol and drug abuse rehabilitation hospital in Riverton, Wyoming, which was about 200 miles from Laramie. I was apparently one of the few "celebrities" in Wyoming at the time, so they hired me. Go figure! But what a great gig that was, aside from the commute. They had me doing TV commercials for them, hosting cocktail parties, and going on the road for various engagements. Cocktail parties, for an alcohol rehab center! I didn't complain, because between making money working on the subdivision in Greeley and at the rehab hospital in Riverton, I was making some pretty good dough. I suppose it was a little ironic that I was working for a rehab center, considering I liked to have a few drinks, along with the pain medications that I still depend upon to this day to manage the pain from 10 years of physical abuse in the NFL.

As I've said, I was pretty full of myself back then, especially when it came to women. I had a big ego. I mean, I didn't go out looking to get in trouble, but if trouble was there, I didn't head in the other direction. I didn't have to take these girls out to dinner and dancing. I would just ask them, "Hey, you wanna go back to the hotel and…?" and they would. It felt great, but when I went home to my wife I didn't necessarily feel so good about it. But I still had the gladiator mentality, and that justified it in my mind. It was like that movie *Spartacus* with Kirk Douglas, when they brought a woman into his cell the night before he had to go into the arena and fight his opponents to the death. I just figured I deserved it.

As it turns out, in May of 1985 I wound up going down to New Orleans for a business trip with the rehab hospital. Little did I know I would meet someone who would change my life forever, a meeting that set me up for more big lessons. One night I went down to the French Quarter for dinner and drinks with the CEO and CFO of the hospital. The two of them fancied themselves as "players" so we went to the famous 544 Club on Bourbon Street. Once we got there, we saw three good-looking ladies who were waiting in line to get in. Well, I knew the owner of the joint from back when I used to play for the Saints, so I asked him if he would please let them in. He obliged and the ladies were very appreciative. We all sat down and started talking. One of the guys asked me, "Why don't you ask the tall gorgeous blonde to dance, so we can hit on the other two?" Hey, the guy was my boss, and I didn't remember receiving a job description, so I figured that must have been in it somewhere.

We started talking and really hit it off. Her name was Joy, and she was a knockout! Joy was a 25-year-old nurse and a single mom from New Iberia, Louisiana, who was in town for the jazz festival. She was a Saints fan too, but she was in nursing school when I had played and really didn't know who I was. Ironically, she had started rooting for the team the year I had left, when the Saints were not doing too well. In fact, Joy and her college friends were some of those fans who started coming to the games with paper bags over their heads and called themselves the "Aints." I thought that was pretty hilarious. Well, one thing led to another and I wound up staying a few extra days down there to hang out with her. Joy didn't know that I was married, and perhaps I led her to believe that I was separated, but we figured we would just have some fun and see where it went.

I was still down there in New Orleans with Joy when I found out that the CEO and CFO, who had returned to Wyoming, had been killed in a horrible drunk driving accident. I couldn't believe it. They were really nice guys and the backbone of the facility. To make matters worse, the fact that the operators of a drug and rehab center were involved in a drunk driving accident did *not* make for good press. As a result, I eventually found myself out of a job in the rehab business.

I was still trying to keep all my plates spinning, and I was going to various charity golf tournaments and other events to make some money. Sometimes Joy would fly to meet me. Everyone knew I was married, so when she showed up at an event in St. Louis, I asked Phil Villipiano—my roommate from Buffalo—to help me out. Well, Joy showed up, a six-foot-tall blonde with a bright red dress on, but Phil was too drunk to go over and act as her date. So I went over to get her myself. We walked back to

According to my parents,
I've been causing trouble
since the day I was born.

I immersed myself in sports
during my high school
days in Twentynine Palms,
California.

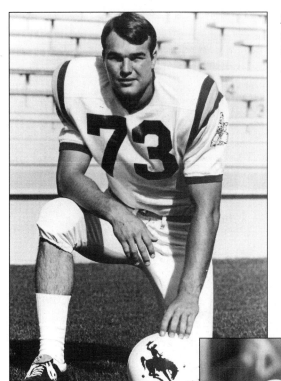

I earned a scholarship to play football at the University of Wyoming in 1968.

The St. Louis Cardinals made me the 110th overall pick in the 1972 NFL Draft.

We had a great offensive line in St. Louis: Dan Dierdorf and Roger Finnie (standing), me and Bob Young (kneeling), and Tom Banks (sitting).

What a couple of good-looking guys! That's me and Tom Banks shopping for some T-shirts.

This Sports Illustrated *cover labeled me "pro football's dirtiest player," a moniker I carry to this very day.*

Hey, I never would have endorsed a product I didn't believe in!

Phyllis George and I shot a segment for the NFL Today show in a local jail cell.

My old coach, Jim Hanifan, speaking at a dinner to "honor" yours truly.

For a couple of years, I worked as a color analyst with Joe McDonald on college football radio broadcasts.

Phil Mickelson, his wife Amy, and Glenn Cohen have been incredibly generous to our daughter Holli and the rest of our family over the years.

Joy and I will continue fighting to advance stem cell research and the rights of retired NFL players.

the table and sat down. Well, there were about 500 people there, and I said, "Phil, do you think anyone noticed us?" He said, "Shit, she's six-feet-tall, blonde, she's in a red dress, she's dressed to the hilt. I think maybe 500 people noticed, but don't worry, I don't think any of the waiters saw because they were all in the kitchen." I figured that it was over, but if any of the other wives questioned me, I was going to say she was with Phil. Oh the evil looks we got!

I figured this was just another plate I would add to my little circus act. If you ever watch the guys in the circus spinning those plates, they have to spend a little bit of time with each one, and that was how I figured I would handle the situation with both Linda and Joy. At the same time, I was trying to keep my various business ventures and income sources going. In those days the housing markets were crashing, and it was a real struggle for me to make ends meet. As a result, I would stay in Greeley during the week by myself to work as much as possible, going back to Laramie to see Linda only on the weekends.

Meanwhile, Joy and I were continuing our long-distance relationship. Our secret meetings went on for a few months, and eventually we both decided to take it to the next level. She started flying up to see me in Greeley and from there one thing led to another. I didn't know what was going to happen, but I was open to just about anything at that point. My ego was definitely out of control. Joy was 10 years younger than I was, and I was totally infatuated with her. She was brilliant and beautiful; when she walked into a room, heads turned. What was not to like? Of course, I felt guilty about all this, and I constantly thought about ways to fix the situation and to refocus on my marriage with Linda. But when I was around Joy at those golf tournaments, I felt pretty damned good about myself. It was kind of a high. In a way, I felt I was kind of addicted to Joy.

Eventually, I realized that I was in love with Joy, and our fling developed into a full-fledged affair. It got so serious that Joy and her son Franco were considering moving to Greeley from New Orleans so we could be closer together. I had all these model homes that were furnished and not being used, so I figured they could live there. My wife was up in Wyoming, and I only went home on Sundays, so why not? There are 60 miles between Greeley and Laramie. I figured I could keep this going until I was forced to make a decision. All I had to do was spend a little time with each plate to keep them all spinning. What could possibly go wrong?

Well, as the saying goes, always be careful what you wish for. My wish came true, and Joy moved from Louisiana in October of 1985. I had promised myself that even though I had been fooling around on Linda, I would never get serious with anyone. But Joy and I were in love with each other. Walking around with this young, good-looking blonde on my arm really fed my ego. It made me feel like I had when I was a football player. In retrospect, my attitude was pretty self-serving.

My feelings were also complicated by economic considerations. Joy had a career as a nurse, and Linda had never worked during our marriage. Now I needed help in paying off debt and supporting my family, and I wasn't getting any from Linda. I suppose there was some resentment on my part, because I was busting my ass to provide for the family. I had helped to put Linda through college, and she hadn't worked at all since those days. Since Joy was working, I figured at least I wouldn't have to pay for rent and food while I was in Greeley. I wasn't proud of being a "kept man," but that's the situation I found myself in.

Just when I thought my life couldn't get any more out of control, Joy and I decided to have a baby. I had adopted my first son, I had the two girls with Linda, and Joy had a son of her own. So why in the hell would I consciously have a baby with another woman while I was still married to somebody else? The honest truth is I have no idea.

Part of me thought she might not even get pregnant. Another part of me though that this would separate me from the herd by making me controversial. I must have been temporarily insane. Maybe I wanted to get caught, I don't know. Maybe I wanted to prove to myself that I could keep up this insane double life that I had created. Maybe I just wanted to live in a world where I could do as I pleased because, as a gladiator, I deserved it. It was pure, out-of-control ego.

At that point, I was basically dividing my time between two women and one of them was my wife. The whole thing was a blur: I would see Joy during the week and then drive 60 miles home to Laramie to see Linda on the weekends. I was living a lie. Plus, the logistics of trying to maintain two households were killing me. I was like one of those Mormon polygamists, juggling two wives. Those guys are my heroes, to be able to keep several women happy at the same time. I thought I was going to have a nervous breakdown, I really did.

One time things got really crazy. A business partner invited Linda and me to his daughter's wedding in Denver. As it turned out, this guy was also fooling around on his wife—with a girl who knew Joy! Well, the guy's girlfriend suggested to Joy that she come on down to the wedding, knowing that Linda would be there. So Joy flies in for the wedding, and I am sitting there with my wife. Of course, Joy knew I was married, but she was under the impression that we were separated, which was true for all practical purposes—or so I had rationalized. I really don't know exactly how she felt, but I guess she just accepted that it was normal for me to be there with my wife and kids at this wedding.

As it turned out, it was my friend's girlfriend who caused a scene at the wedding. She half-heartedly attempted to commit suicide, so Joy came to get me to help out. Linda just thought she was a friend, so things appeared fairly normal to everyone. The girl had a bottle of pills and a bottle of booze, but I don't think she was really trying to kill herself. She just made it look like she had tried to kill herself. She was just being dramatic. I guess she thought that my friend was going to leave his wife at his daughter's wedding to go comfort her. I got over there and I told her, "Look, let's cut the bullshit. Go ahead and wake up because it's not going to happen. It's his daughter's wedding and you may as well just wake up. He's not going to leave his wife to come see you. Now I left my wife there, and I think it was insulting that you invited Joy down when you knew my wife was going to be there."

Meanwhile, as all of this insanity was unfolding in my personal life, my career got a huge shot in the arm when out of the blue I got a phone call from the Miller Brewing Company late in 1986. They wanted me to star in one of their famous Miller Lite commercials! To say I was absolutely thrilled would have been an understatement. The first commercial had me taking a seat between two unsuspecting fans at a ballgame, introducing myself as a "troublemaker," but confessing that deep down I was really just a "nice guy" who liked to watch a game with a cold Miller Lite.

I then proceeded to entice the two fans into a "Tastes great! Less filling!" argument, with both sides of the bleachers getting into the action. While they were going at it, I reappeared a few seconds later in another section of the stadium and got another argument started between two different fans drinking beers. It was really funny. They had rented out Giants Stadium for our shoot. The whole thing took about five hours and involved around 40 takes. I was so nervous, I even brought in a bunch of my buddies to help me practice my lines over and over. Needless to say, we drank a shitload of Miller Lite! It was a neat experience and the finished product was great.

The campaign was so successful that I was asked to come back the following year as part of a group of ex-jocks—including Bubba Smith, Dick Butkus, and Bob Uecker—a "who's who" of the sports world. In the ad, we were all dressed up like cowboys sitting around a campfire in the middle of the desert. All of a sudden, a flying saucer lands, and none other than legendary comedian Rodney Dangerfield gets out, along with a whole bunch of Rodney clones, and they scare everybody away. It was hilarious! We filmed it out in Culver City, California, and it took about four days to shoot. It was a blast hanging around with so many interesting people, telling stories, and drinking Miller Lite beer.

Rodney was an interesting guy to say the least. I thought he was going to be this big party guy and want to hang out with all of us, but he pretty much stayed in his trailer by himself all the time. He would come out for shoots and that was about it. On camera he was hilarious, but off camera he was kind of a jerk. You think you know someone from their Hollywood persona, but when you meet them it is more often than not a big letdown. I suppose I was the same as Rodney, a person with a persona, except with Rodney it was a character he played, whereas I had actually bought into my persona.

The funny thing about doing those Miller Lite commercials is that it gave me a level of notoriety I had never known before. During my entire NFL career, I barely got noticed in my hometown of Twentynine Palms, California. I remember going home shortly after the commercial came out, however, and there was a mob of people wanting my autograph. Guys bought me beers, and women wanted me to autograph various parts of their bodies! It was crazy. You play professional football for 10 seasons and obtain a level of recognition amongst your peers that you feel pretty good about. Then all of a sudden you make a beer commercial, five hours of work, and you are an American hero. How messed up is that? If I had known then what I know now, I would have skipped football altogether and gone straight to Hollywood! Later, I even got a job working for Miller, making public appearances throughout the country as a "Miller Lite All-Star." It was so much fun to be walking down the street or sitting in a restaurant and have random people yell "Tastes great!" just so I could yell back "Less filling!" That just fed my inflated ego; it was like throwing gasoline on a fire.

The best part about doing that first commercial was that it gave me a reprieve from the train wreck that my personal life had become. Getting away from it all for a while was a godsend. I remember sitting around talking to all of these former pro athletes, drinking beer, and talking about my situation back home. The guys were blown away. They couldn't believe what I was up to, and they were amazed at how I kept all the plates spinning. As expected though, some plates would have to come crashing down. It was like I had taken a few steps down a path and I didn't know where it was leading me. Then, after a few more steps, I found myself on a completely different path than the one I thought I was on, and I realized I really did not know how to turn around. Joy was pregnant, and so I decided that I had to come clean with Linda.

I remember the night well. It was sometime in November of 1986. I took Linda out to dinner at a nice new restaurant in Laramie called Frinfrock's, figuring she couldn't kill me in front of all the other customers. She looked pretty nice, and I had a few scotches to give me courage. Linda was drinking a glass of wine, and she asked me what I was still doing in Greeley now that the subdivision had already closed. "Well," I said, "I met someone." She just looked at me and said, "Oh, really?" I said, "Yeah, really." Then I added, "And she's pregnant." It was like I had punched Linda in the stomach. She really couldn't say anything at first. Finally, she looked at me and said, "What is fucking wrong with you?"

At that moment our dinners arrived, and Linda just got up and left the restaurant. The waiter asked, "Is she coming back?" I answered, "I don't think so." I asked the waiter to give me the bill and told him to give the food to the dishwashers. We were right in the middle of a snowstorm, and so I had to go out and find Linda. I pulled up next to her in the car and begged her to please get inside. She was crying, but finally she got in the car and I drove her home. We talked on the drive, and I was feeling lower than whale shit. She couldn't understand how I could do this to our beautiful children. I did not know what to say. It's not like you can prepare a speech for this kind of thing. I dropped her at home, told her we should talk tomorrow, and I went and checked into a hotel. The next day I came over and she asked what I was going to do. I loved Linda and I loved Joy, but I knew the best thing that I could do in order to take care of Abbey, Erin, Mark, and the new baby on the way was to stay with Joy. To be clear, though, I mostly decided to stay with Joy because I saw her love as a gift and did not act only out of obligation.

Hurting Linda like that was one of the worst moments of my life. I felt terrible about the whole thing because she hadn't done anything wrong. It was all me. I was the egotistical asshole. She is a wonderful, wonderful person and a great lady. How she put up with me for all those years I will never know. The woman is a saint. Anyway, she took the news pretty badly, as expected, and at that point we both knew that our marriage was over. I felt bad about that, but I knew that I was doing the right thing. Linda and I later went to see a psychologist, not to reconcile but to help with the transition for our kids. We needed help on how to explain a complicated situation to them. Well, the psychologist really went after me! Between the two of them, they really let me have it, tag-teaming me left and right and telling me what an asshole I was. I was pissed, but I just took my medicine. I really got what I deserved from them.

That same year, with my financial situation deteriorating, I decided that I had to declare bankruptcy, and then Linda and I started the divorce proceedings a short while later. In the end I didn't want to dump anything on Linda, so I basically gave her everything. I wanted to do whatever I could to help her and the kids. I was going to be starting over in life and didn't want to burden them with my mistakes. But because of the bankruptcy, things got complicated. We lost our house in the process, but I was able to buy another one for Linda and the kids so that they weren't inconvenienced. I also made arrangements to pay for her to get her master's degree, too.

Linda would later get remarried to a really nice, quiet guy—the complete opposite of me—and became very successful, which is wonderful. In fact, today she is in charge of the entire mental health program for the state for Wyoming. Shit, now she is making more than I am. Hey, she deserves it. Maybe I should request some type of compensation, since I gave her so much experience with how to deal with difficult people?

To this day, I feel awful about everything I put Linda through. I am not proud of it. In fact, I still wear a ring that Linda gave me 21 years ago. She is the mother of my three children, and I will always respect her. I hope I will never again hurt anyone the way I hurt Linda. Looking back, I realize that buying into my gladiator persona was a big reason my marriage failed. Many NFL players see their marriages fail for this same reason. I was also starting to finally learn that I could only keep plates spinning for so long before some of them crashed to the ground.

6

A NEW BEGINNING

*"It's remarkable
how little things
can change the entire direction
of your life."*

In early 1987, I had begun to accept that perhaps I was, in fact, *not* infallible. I was *not* Superman. I could *not* fly. I could *not* have my cake and eat it, too. I started to realize that the self-image that I had bought into so completely was not always going to insulate me from the negative consequences of my actions. That realization marked the start of a new beginning for me. It was one of those moments in life where you see things clearly for the first time. My mistakes had helped me learn a lot about myself, and I had decided to make some changes, to try to do things right. I felt a tremendous sense of responsibility to Linda and our children, as well as to Joy, who was pregnant with our first child, Holli. In spite of the mess I had made of my personal life, at least I was able to make sure that everyone was taken care of. It seemed that I had won a major battle at that point—the gladiator's battle with himself. And while I was sorry about having hurt Linda and for whatever difficulties our divorce had put the kids through, it was a real relief to finally stop living a lie, and I looked forward to starting my family and my new life with Joy. The next decade would present its share of difficult challenges, but we were in for a lot of good times, too. It would be like a roller coaster, with the bottom dropping out suddenly at times, only to rise back to a new height each time.

Joy and I leased a house in Ft. Collins, Colorado. At that time, I was still in the process of going through the divorce, finding housing for Linda and our kids, dealing with Linda and the psychologists for the kids, going to Lamaze classes with Joy, studying for my real estate exam, and to top it off the Miller Lite folks had me out on the promotional speaking circuit, traveling around the country and talking to their distributors and various clients. I still had a lot of plates to keep spinning, and it was kind of a crazy time. At least with the income from Miller Lite, I was back making pretty good money. That was a relief, of course; with all the mouths I had to feed, I really needed the extra income!

Traveling around and working for Miller Lite was a lot of fun. People enjoyed my un–politically correct sense of humor and I was a big hit. One year I did 80 engagements for them, so they kept me pretty busy. Sometimes they would fly me first class, pick me up in limos, and put me up in five-star hotels. I was rolling high again! But Joy wasn't enjoying her job very much at the time, so that caused a little tension in our relationship just as we were starting out. After all, Joy is a very competent person, had been a star basketball player in school, and was used to being in the limelight, so it may have been hard for her to watch me enjoying myself. At the same time, we both realized that the income from the Miller Lite engagements was a very good thing. I also knew that I had to be careful not to get too full of myself again. I think I was starting to realize that there are some positive aspects to the gladiator mentality that you don't want to necessarily get rid of; it's sometimes good to feel invincible. It keeps you motivated and focused on success in the face of adversity. I just had to remember to keep it in moderation.

You might be surprised to hear that drinking beer all day for a living was actually pretty tough to do! The truth is that I was not a big beer drinker. Sure, Miller Lite is a great beer. (It tastes great, *and* it's less filling!) But personally, I much prefer to drink scotch. Sometimes I would secretly dump out my beer, just to make it look like I was keeping up with everybody else. After all, I had this image of being a big, tough ex-jock who drank beer all day, and I had to play the part. I took it very seriously, though, and I worked my ass off and really did a good job for Miller Lite.

I would stay out until 2:00 in the morning entertaining clients, telling stories and doing whatever they asked of me.

Meanwhile, Joy gave birth to our daughter, Holli Dai Dobler, on April 28, 1987. We had been through a lot that past year and we were really excited to start a new family together. We weren't married at this point, however, and that was starting to bug Joy. Of course, my divorce from Linda wasn't finalized until January of 1988. At that point Holli's first birthday was coming up, and so Joy said, facetiously, "Are we going to wait until she's in college to get married?" Around that time, Joy and Linda had gotten together to discuss the logistics of having stepchildren. In the process, they actually wound up becoming friends. How crazy is that? Now my wife and my ex-wife were together and talking about me, analyzing my shortcomings, and comparing notes.

Joy and I finally got married in February of 1988. It was not an elaborate ceremony, just a small gathering in Phoenix to make it official. I am very public in some things, yet very private in others. This was private to me. I didn't want anybody judging me for what I had done, but then again I don't really care about what other people think, anyway. But I didn't even invite my parents to the wedding. Hell, they didn't even know I was getting married or that they had a new granddaughter! I had not told my parents that Joy was pregnant because I wanted to wait until after Joy and I had gotten married.

The important thing is that I felt good about myself, because even though I had messed up with Linda, I felt staying with Joy had been the right decision. I knew it was the right thing to do. One of the main beliefs of the Catholic Church is redemption through confession of your sins. Of course, there was the time when I was a kid and went to confession, and I actually lied to the priest in the confessional box! I had gone in to confess my sins, and I told the priest that I had missed Mass one Sunday. Well, I just expected to receive a penance and be on my way; I didn't expect him to question me. So, when he asked me, "Why did you miss Mass?" I made up a lie. I told him my brother and I didn't have a car, but the truth was we had just decided not to go because my parents were out of town. I remember walking out of there thinking, *Wait a minute, what did I just do?*

Anyway, I have learned from my mistakes that it is best to always tell the truth; that way you don't have to remember what you've said. I just wanted to own up to my past mistakes, get married to Joy, and get on with my life, free of guilt. Of course, I will always regret the birthdays, sports events, proms, and graduations I missed with my kids. I will always feel remorseful that I abandoned Mark, Erin, and Abbey, that I should have been a better dad. That is a burden I will have to carry until the day I die. So I had made my decisions, and I had to live with the consequences. I'll never feel completely guilt free for my past mistakes; I can only try to do better *now*.

For a while, things were humming along just fine. My life with Joy was really good. I would bring up the kids from Laramie every other weekend to stay with us and we just made it work. Joy and Linda were great about all of that stuff, which made my life a lot easier. Joy and I were genuinely happy at that time, especially after our second child, Stephen, was born on July 1, 1989. I now had two families with three kids each. The six kids kind of settled into becoming brothers and sisters very easily, and there was not much tension at all. I felt like I had come through the worst possible experience I could imagine and that things were going to be okay. I didn't realize it at the time, but the "little tornadoes" that I had survived would pale in comparison to the turbulent future in store for me and Joy.

After a couple years of smooth sailing, things started to get rocky again when my gig with Miller Lite ended—all because of that damn Budweiser dog, Spuds McKenzie. With that campaign, Bud started kicking Miller's ass, and as a result, Miller decided to cancel the entire "Tastes great! Less filling!" campaign. (That campaign had been the longest, most successful advertising campaign in TV commercial history, lasting about 15 years.) To make things worse, the real estate market was in flux and all of my investments had tanked. Suddenly, we found ourselves really struggling again financially and trying to figure out what to do next. It was stressful, but I had not completely lost my self-confidence. I had always performed without a safety net, and I always knew that I would bounce back higher than before.

Just when I didn't know what to do next, along came a book deal with a very handsome advance of $125,000. Because of the publicity I had gotten from the Miller Lite ads and public engagements, I got the chance to write *They Call Me Dirty* with Vic Carucci, whom I had met in Buffalo when playing for the Bills. The book was full of all sorts of hilarious stories about my playing days. Once it came out, we scheduled a book tour. The additional exposure eventually led to me doing other keynote and after-dinner speaking engagements for other groups and companies. This was enough for Joy and I to finally buy our own house in Fort Collins. We only received half of the advance, and I had to split that with Vic, so with taxes and two households to pay for, it didn't last very long. If I hadn't done the Miller Lite commercials, the book deal would never have happened. In fact, in the photo on the cover of the book, I am wearing the same vest I wore in the Miller Lite commercial. Sometimes one thing leads to another when you least expect it.

As luck would have it, I was heading out to play golf one day when I got a call out of the blue from KCMO, a radio station in Kansas City, asking me to do an interview. Now, I had done a lot of radio interviews before, many of them to promote the book, and I was used to doing these interviews over the phone. So when they said that they wanted to fly me to Kansas City for the interview, I sort of laughed at them. I thought, *Why in the hell would they want me to fly all the way to Kansas City to do an interview that we could do over the phone?* I figured these guys must have had more money than brains. In fact, I was actually pretty rude to them, almost belittling them for asking such a stupid question. When they asked me if I would speak with them that day, I sort of arrogantly brushed them off. I said, "I'm on my way out the door to play golf, call me back in a few days." The truth is that I don't like to be late for anything, even a tee time.

Well, the guys at KCMO called me back a few days later and asked if I had a few minutes to talk, so I said sure. This time, however, the vice president of Gannett Radio was on the phone. I thought that was sort of odd for just a run-of-the mill radio interview. It was at that point that it finally dawned on me what was going on: they didn't want to interview me on the air, they wanted to interview me for a job at their radio station as the host of my own show. Once I figured that out, I emphatically apologized. This was a real opportunity.

Gannett Radio flew me down to Kansas City to meet with the KCMO staff, and we hit it off right away. The departing host of the show had just taken a job in Los Angeles. His name was Ed "Superfan" Beiler, and apparently he was an early "shock jock" kind of a guy. He had great ratings though, so they wanted to replace him with someone who they felt was also pretty controversial. Basically, they wanted an asshole like me who would say whatever was on his mind and would not be afraid to stir up some shit. I guess based on our first phone conversation, they thought I was definitely their guy! Ironically, it was my bad attitude on that first phone call that actually landed me the job. They offered me a three-year contract with a $125,000 annual salary, on the spot, to host an afternoon call-in show. They were actually going to pay me to talk on the radio for a couple hours a day. I couldn't believe it. What a country!

It's remarkable how little things can change the entire direction of your life. I got my start in the NFL because a guy lost his chin strap. Now I was getting this great radio gig because I had insulted the people that wanted to interview me for the job because of a misunderstanding. Sometimes, I guess, even your mistakes can accidentally lead to unexpected good things.

After signing on with Gannett and KCMO, though, I remember telling Joy that I was a little nervous about the new job and that I was wondering if I had made the right decision. Joy said, "Well, you didn't know anything about writing books, did you? And you wrote a book, right? And you didn't know anything about acting, and you did several Miller Lite commercials, right? Well, you've done a lot of public speaking, so what could be so difficult about talk radio?" As usual, she was absolutely right. That was exactly the pep talk that I needed.

I have always considered myself to be a very shy, sensitive, and somewhat insecure person, really. The fear of failure has often motivated me to prove that I was just as good as everybody else; it has motivated me to succeed. Of course, sometimes just a few words of encouragement from someone who cares about you can make a really big difference. Joy had reminded me of my skills and my experience and encouraged me to believe in myself and my abilities.

I was now excited about getting into the radio business, and I moved down to Kansas City by myself in September of 1989 to start the show. Joy had stayed in Ft. Collins with the kids for a while until I got settled in Kansas City, and I had been on the air for a few weeks when Joy and the kids moved out to join me. I will never forget the day they flew out to meet the moving van at our new home in Kansas City. I got home from the radio station that evening, and Joy told me that our new neighbor had come over and introduced herself. She was an elderly lady who must have been in her seventies at the time and a sports fan who had been listening to me on my radio show. She said, "You must be the new neighbor. Your husband is Conrad, right?" Joy said yes, and then the lady said, "Well, you know, I really listen to a lot of radio, and I have heard your husband's show, and frankly, I don't know if you should be unpacking all those boxes. I don't think he's going to make it!"

Well, we unpacked the boxes, of course. It took Joy a while to find the right job, and after a bad experience with one company, she took a job in the nurse staffing business, working for her ex-boyfriend from college. I really had to swallow my pride hard on that one, but I loved Joy and didn't want to act like a jealous husband. I was really trying to be mature about it all. Joy had a child when I met her, so I figured she probably wasn't a virgin. I also figured that I am Conrad Dobler, so why would she cheat on me with this short, chubby guy? I guess I was a little insecure about it, but I decided that I would trust Joy and behave myself, too.

Besides, we needed the extra income to help pay off a debt to the IRS that we had accrued from the advance that I had received for *They Call Me Dirty.* In fact, the IRS actually came to my house one day—with badges and guns—to remind me that they wanted their money. I owed them around $18,000, but when they finished up with me I had to pay them $58,000. I had taken my time paying them off because a couple years earlier the IRS owed me about $40,000, and it took me two years to get my money from them. So I figured, turnabout is fair play. I figured wrong! The IRS doesn't care about fair play. I was pretty angry and defensive when they showed up at my house, and I asked one IRS agent where the hell he thought my kids would live if they took my house away. He just looked me in the eye and said, "The IRS doesn't care where your damn kids live," and then he flashed the gun that he had on his hip. I guess the lesson here is that it just is not smart to argue with the IRS.

Once we worked things out with the IRS, things started to come together again. I felt like we had been through the worst of it and had come out okay. The kids were situated in school, and we had made some new friends. I wasn't able to see my children from my first marriage as often as I wanted, and that was really tough. The kids were really super about everything though. I am really blessed to have such great children.

Needless to say, I struggled in the beginning to get acclimated to my new job as a drive-time talk-show host. I ultimately worked at KCMO for three years, but I was never really great at it. I thought it was going to be one of the easiest jobs I ever had, but it turned out to be one of the toughest. At first I was excited about working in a new market and to be doing something totally new and interesting, but I had no training or experience being a broadcaster. They just shoved a microphone in front of me, and the "ON AIR" light came on! I had the personality they were looking for and I could certainly talk, but there are certain skills and knowledge required to do radio properly that I did not have at the time.

Also, for the first two and a half years or so, I was alone in the booth, with no co-host to talk to and no audience in front of me. I had never performed without an audience before, so it was a very awkward and uncomfortable experience to be alone talking to a microphone. Of course, the people in Kansas City are big Chiefs fans, and they didn't really give a damn that I had been a St. Louis Cardinal. Our station was the home of the Chiefs, but we only had one year left on the broadcast contract, and the Royals' baseball games were broadcast on another station. I was not a baseball fan, but when you are on the air five days a week, year-round, you need to talk about the other sports, too.

To me, watching baseball was like watching paint dry, and because I wasn't a fan, I was never afraid to really go after the players when they weren't playing well. Hell, I didn't care. I just wanted to stir things up. Fans would call in and chew me out, at which point I would scream right back at them. I guess I was kind of like Howard Stern...only better look-ing! It wasn't really my personality, just this "shock jock" persona that I was trying to create. I learned that it was easy to be an actor if you have a pretty face, but it was difficult to be an actor on the radio. You have to fill more than just the camera lens. In radio you really have to find your own course; it doesn't really work if you just copy someone else.

I remember one day driving in my car and pulling up to a stop light. I look over, and in the car next to me was Chiefs kicker Jan Stenerud. He said, "Conrad, hang in there, you are doing a great job!" That meant a lot to me. Jan was inducted into the Pro Football Hall of Fame years later. What a classy guy he is. I had been so lonely cooped up in that damn booth, to get some positive feedback and encouragement like that was very nice.

I quickly learned that it was harder to do a call-in show if the Chiefs or Royals had won because nobody called in, and you actually had to work to come up with content to fill the void. But when the teams lost, it was a different story all together. All you had to do then was sit back and listen to all the fans who called in to bitch. After a while, it was like torture listening to all of these idiots call in day after day, talking about the same old bullshit over and over. I will never forget frequently battling with one caller, "Ernest from Excelsior Springs." I will never forget that clown's name. It's emblazoned on my brain, I think. That guy would call in every day to complain about Royals third baseman George Brett. Give me a break!

After a while I started getting truly pissed off at a lot of the callers, and the line between persona and person was blurred. I remember one time a guy called in and he was so depressed about the Chiefs that he was actually considering committing suicide, and I said, "Go for it! Do it, man! Make a statement!" People thought I was crazy. Another time I cracked a joke that some people considered to be in pretty poor taste, and that got me in a bit of trouble. The joke was: "What do you call a Jewish kid who isn't a lawyer? A doctor." Well, that seemed harmless enough to me, but the Jewish Anti-Defamation League got on me, and I caught hell for it. But I was an equal opportunity offender, including many of our sponsors—which didn't go over well with the corporate brass. I even got into a pretty heated shouting match with a guy who claimed to be a mobster in town, challenging him to come down to the station and shoot me. It was nuts.

Every now and then a listener would call up and try to trick me on the air. I remember one guy tried to fool me by asking something like, "Well, do you think that the Cardinals and the Phillies could ever meet in the World Series?" Now, I had a young intern back there who was supposed to be feeding me the right answers for this type of thing, but I wasn't thinking and just blurted out, "Yeah, that's a possibility." Well, obviously there's no way they can meet in the World Series, because they are both in the National League. The listener then got all excited and screamed out, "You dumb sonofabitch, what are you doing radio for?" I was smart enough to think on my feet though, so I said, "Oh yeah? Well, have you ever heard of realignment?" I had read about realignment someplace and really had no idea what it meant, but it was a great comeback on the air. I said, "You asked me if they could 'ever meet.' Well, with realignment there is a possibility that they could meet in the World Series." I then looked over at my damn intern and said, "Why didn't you tell me they were in the same fucking league!" and he said, "Well, you're the sports guy! Don't you know?" I didn't know; I was a football guy! I couldn't even name all the football teams, let alone all the baseball teams.

In three years of doing radio, I think the most important contribution that I ever made was that day in 1990 when Iraq invaded Kuwait. I was usually in the studio by myself between 3:00 in the afternoon and 7:00 in the evening; everything I needed was on tape. Everyone else had left for the day, and I was alone in the news room when the news broke. I had to go to CNN. I had to go to NBC, CBS, and all the rest until the news people got in there and took over. For those few moments, while I was on the air, I felt like I was actually doing something that was fucking important. Because in reality, sports are not a cure for cancer or spinal cord injuries; they are just sports. It's just a game. If the Chiefs win or lose, if the Royals win or lose, no one is going to die; the sun is going to come up tomorrow. I could never understand how people could get so bent out of shape about this stuff. Anyway, that was my big moment, and it was neat to have that experience and to feel as if I actually did something of substance on the radio.

Eventually, I just got tired of the entire lifestyle, and it became boring and torturous. When we lost the rights to broadcast Chiefs games in the second year, there was a lot less football to talk about, and we lost a lot of our listeners. I did get to do a Chiefs postgame show once a week during football season which was fun, and I knew a lot about the Chiefs from my days in nearby St. Louis, so it came pretty easily for me. In fact, I had played in the inaugural game at Arrowhead Stadium in Kansas City, Missouri, and there was always this rivalry between the Cardinals and the Chiefs. We would compete in exhibition games against Kansas City for the Missouri Governor's Cup, but nobody really gave a damn about that. Hell, I never even saw the trophy, and it could have stayed in Jefferson City for all we cared. We wanted a Super Bowl ring.

But some days I would come in and it was like four hours of torture, especially during the baseball season. It was like being water-boarded. After a while they wanted me to start ripping on the local star athletes to start controversies in order to boost ratings. I would almost have to make shit up just to get the phones to ring. My heart wasn't into it.

In the last year of my contract, they had me working with a guy named Bob Mayhall, who actually had a degree in broadcasting and who worked at the station as an intern. He was really good, and he taught me a lot about radio broadcasting. He was just supposed to be my producer, but I slowly wove him into the booth. I used to have a lot of fun with Bob. If we ever got stumped and there were no phone calls coming in, I would ask him what he thought about whatever I was talking about, and he would go into this big long monologue, with his radio knowledge, doing a really eloquent job. Then I would stop him and say, "Now wait a minute here. Do you really think that anyone listening really cares what *you* think? You are *nobody*." When we got really disrespectful with each other, and especially toward some of the fans who would call in, our ratings started to go way up. A fan would call in, for example, and I would say, "Well, you're an idiot," or "Only an idiot would say that," and people were eating it up.

Even though our ratings had climbed, they told me that my contract wasn't going to be renewed in 1992. In the radio business, that's the easy way of saying you got fired. I wasn't having much fun at that point anyway. Ironically, once I found out that I was going to be let go, I was able to just relax and have fun. As a result, our ratings really started to go through the roof. We were talking about some really raunchy stuff and just getting crazy on the air. It was actually quite liberating. We pulled within half a point of the No. 2 spot in the entire market, which would mean that they had to pay me a bonus, which would have been a nice parting gift. I guess it was too little, too late, because for me the show was over. I have never had a chance to work in radio like that since.

While working at KCMO, I got a side gig working as a color analyst with this national radio broadcasting group out of Chicago. They would do the "college game of the week" and it was really exciting. I would fly out on Friday night, do the game on Saturday, and then fly back on Sunday. I was doing some big games and it was a lot of fun—Auburn vs. Alabama, UCLA vs. USC, and Notre Dame vs. Michigan. College football is so much more exciting than what you see at a professional football game. There is so much excitement around a college football game. The student body is excited, the fans are excited, and the players are excited. The unexpected really happens in college football games. A professional game is almost like scripted theater compared to college; very few mistakes are made. In college football, mistakes are made, big plays are made, and things happen that are unexpected.

The only bad part about doing the college games on radio was I had to work with a real professional by the name of Joe McDonald. Joe was a great guy and a good, professional broadcaster, but he was from the old school. He wasn't used to working alongside somebody else and would rather just do everything by himself. It was nearly impossible to get a word in edgewise with the guy. He was a real piece of work. Usually the play-by-play guy and the color guy will talk back and forth about things, like they are having a conversation while watching the game. But with Joe, it was like I was doing a game, and he was doing a game— separately. He never said anything like, "That's a good point, Conrad." I would describe things sometimes, but he would never respond to them. He would just go on to the next thing.

Sometimes when I would say something, Joe would roll his finger at me as a signal to shut up and throw it back to him. Well, that really pissed me off. It frazzled me too, which made me lose my train of thought. Finally, I said, "If you wag that finger at me one more time, I am going to break the sonofabitch right off." Needless to say, he let me express myself a little bit more after that. I wound up calling games for about two years until the company went broke. It was too bad because I really enjoyed doing it.

Around the time I lost the KCMO contract, my dad died. I was pretty upset about it. My sister Cindy had died a year earlier, which had also been very difficult. My dad and I weren't real close, but he meant a lot to me. Now, when I look back at my childhood and I remember how hard my parents worked and the things they valued, I understand where my own work ethic and my whole way of living and looking at life comes from. I surely resemble my dad in a lot of ways. He never graduated from high school, flunking his final exam in English his senior year. I never finished up my college degree (and to this day, I regret not finishing that task). He had six children, and so do I. He started his own business and worked at it all his life, just like I do now, and my dad worked until the day he died. He was always there to help someone who needed help. He was a remarkable man. Looking back, I realize that time spent with your family is one of the most important things in life. I wish I had spent more time with my dad and that I could have told him just once before he died that I loved him.

I remember being at the funeral and listening to the bishop read the eulogy. At one point, he said, "John had one son who was a CPA, another son who is a mayor, and another son who was a football." Maybe he meant to say "in football," but he didn't say that. He didn't say "a football player," either. He just said "a football." I was sitting there and just started laughing to myself. How do you like that? I am "a football." Here I am, a former Pro Bowl player, and I am reduced to being "a football." That sort of summed up my life, right then and there. Even though football is a beautiful part of my life and I enjoyed the hell out of it, there is a lot more to me than just being a dumb fucking jock.

So after my radio career was over in 1992, I was out of a job. I was still paying child support, I had three children and an ex-wife out in Wyoming, and I had a wife and three children with me in Kansas City. I had absolutely no idea what we were going to do. I thought that if we moved to St. Louis where I used to play, I could hook onto something there. Fortunately, Joy was still working (with her ex-boyfriend) in the health staffing business. She was doing so well that she lined up a bunch of clients, and she took the company's revenues from a few hundred thousand a year to over $1 million in annual sales. She started making a bunch of money on commissions, she was flying around the country, and she had become the main breadwinner for the family. That was great, but it was not necessarily great for my ego. I was proud of her but needed to find my own career. As it turned out, after Joy landed all those clients, they wanted to give her a promotion, and they asked her to sign a non-compete agreement. Well, she had been making about $80,000 a year, so after she had ramped up their revenues, they found someone to take over her office for only $30,000 per year, asked her to sign a non-compete agreement, and then fired her.

When they fired Joy, I said, "Well, I don't have a job, and you don't have a job. What do you think we should do?" We were kind of looking at each other, and I said to her, "Well, I'm really good at raising money, and you know this nurse staffing business. Why don't we just start our own company?" So in January of 1993, we started our own business, Superior Health Care Staffing, out of our house. We got a couple nurses and a couple of contracts, enough to keep us going, and we built it from there.

We worked all day long and were on call 24 hours a day, seven days a week. We would start our day around 4:00 in the morning, which was when the hospitals started calling. There were times when Joy and I were working so much in the mornings that we did not even have time to change out of our pajamas. Every night we would sit down, have a cocktail, and each make about 20 cold calls looking for more nurses. We would pay our kids, who were in grade school then, about 2¢ for each phone number they got out of the city directory. Out of 40 calls each night, we would usually get a couple new nurses for our staff. After a while, we were really pumping people out.

As we continued to grow the business, we ran into a little cash-flow problem, so I went to the bank to ask for a $100,000 asset-based loan. The only problem was that I had no assets, and they would only lend me $15,000. Within two weeks I went back and got another $15,000. Then a few weeks later I borrowed another $15,000, then another $15,000 a few weeks after that. Finally the banker said, "You have come in here five times in the last two months." I said "Well, two months ago, I came in here and asked you for $100,000. I told you what we were going to do, and you wouldn't give it to me. I showed you the projections. You're the businessman. What are you bitchin' at me for? You should be happy that my business is growing."

When times were tough, we had had to borrow some money from Joy's friend and also from her brother. But within three months of starting our business, we had paid everyone back. We worked hard to build the company, and we ended up with a $1 million line of credit. We had about 20 or 30 nurses. We were so busy that sometimes we'd be getting the kids ready for school and one of the nurses would be there having breakfast in our house, fixing them a bowl of cereal and helping us get them out the door.

On weekends, we'd be relaxing when the cell phone would ring. The kids would yell "The phone! The phone!" and we would have to jump out of the pool and run to the phone. They knew that we had to answer the phone when it rang because it was a hospital calling for a nurse. Our kids weren't working on the docks or anything, but it was their responsibility to make sure that we always got the phone before it stopped ringing, because we had to be available 24/7. It was kind of like High Desert Delivery Service all over again. So we worked and worked and worked, and after many years of great effort we had found success. And then one day we were hit by "the perfect storm."

7

THE PERFECT STORM

"Joy said, 'I can't feel my feet.'
So I said, 'It's probably just a pinched nerve.'
She said, 'No, I heard something snap.
I think I broke my neck,
so don't anyone move me.'"

Everyone has trials and tribulations in his or her life, ups and downs, wins and losses. The bad times can sometimes be severe and difficult to weather. Hopefully, they are spread out enough over time so that you have enough strength and resources to deal with each obstacle as it comes at you. Occasionally, however, some of life's major challenges seem to come all at the same time or one right after the other, and you can find yourself caught in the middle of "the perfect storm". That is what happened to our family starting in 2001.

A real perfect storm is caused by natural weather events that converge only once every hundred years or so. In life, sometimes the perfect storm is caused by the actions of the people who are caught in the middle of it, sometimes not, but the effects are never fully known until the people are out of the storm. Those of us who have been caught in a perfect storm didn't choose to be caught in it. But when we find ourselves in the middle of one, all of our previous challenges seem like exhibition games. Everything in your life is on the line, and you have to reach inside yourself and find an inner strength that you never knew you had.

By 2001, Joy and I had survived some very difficult moments over the 16 years or so that we had been together. It had been a real roller-coaster ride at times, and we had to weather several "little tornadoes" over the years. But somehow we had pushed through and it seemed we were finally coming out on top. We had worked through all the major difficulties that life had presented to us, and after years of hard work and a lot of determination and perseverance, we were doing very well.

Superior Health Care Staffing eventually got so big that we were able to buy our own office building. In 1996, the business was doing so well that we decided to borrow against our new house, expand the business to other cities, and try to take our company public. Things were going great until we decided to bring on a couple of people that had some corporate experience, which ended up being a big mistake. These corporate guys opened offices in Houston, Texas, and Tallahassee, Florida, and so we ended up with a corporate staff of 17 people across all our locations, but we probably only needed half that many. Our field staff numbered around 200 nurses and other health care professionals. Because of management problems in the expansion offices, the revenues we needed to realize a profit were never achieved. None of those offices were profitable, and instead they ramped up our costs, marking the start of our dangerous downward spiral.

Even though we were up against the ropes, I remained focused on achieving success. Joy and I had weathered other storms before, and we were fully preparing to fight through this one, too. I understood that it would take time to bring revenues up to the level we needed to support our new overhead. The problem was the managers we had hired to oversee the new offices were ineffective in recruiting field staff or placing them in revenue-making positions.

Everything had been going so well. How could it all fall apart so fast? We had no clue that our problems were really just beginning. Realizing we were in serious trouble, we found ourselves in a desperate fight to save the business that we had worked so hard to build from scratch. We decided to consult with a recruiting firm that screened their applicants with detailed tests, and they recommended someone to start immediately on July 1, 2001.

But on July 4, 2001, a freak accident would occur that would change our world forever. That was the day that Joy fell out of the hammock.

My mother was about to celebrate her 80th birthday on July 7, so we were all getting ready to fly out on July 5 to celebrate with her in California. We were out by the pool in our backyard and had been playing volleyball with the kids. Some friends were over too, including a business associate named Larry Hall. Larry had gone over and gotten into the hammock with his girlfriend. I was up on the deck cooking lamb loins.

We were all looking forward to having this really nice dinner when my son Stephen, who had just turned 12 a few days earlier, came running up to me and said, "Dad, Mom thinks she broke her neck." I thought he was joking with me, but he said, "No Dad, Mom *really* thinks she broke her neck." So I ran down there and Joy was lying on the grass. Larry and his girlfriend were down on the ground next to her. I didn't know *what* was going on. I thought maybe she had one of those stingers you get in football, like a pinched nerve that lasts a few minutes or something. After all, the hammock was only one or two feet off the ground. Joy said, "I can't feel my feet." So I said, "It's probably just a pinched nerve." She said, "No, I heard something snap. I think I broke my neck, so don't anyone move me."

Well, I called an ambulance immediately to take Joy to the hospital. My eldest son, Mark, my daughter Abby, and the two grandkids had just left to drive back to Colorado, and my other kids were out somewhere, either with friends or off shooting fireworks. I went to the hospital with Joy, and I was in the waiting room not really knowing what was going on. I don't think I ever thought that Joy was going to die, but I didn't know enough about her injury to fully realize the serious implications.

We had been having such a nice day, and I felt terrible that it had ended this way, but I did not realized how serious the situation really was. While waiting to see Joy in the ER, I called all the children, not really knowing what to say. Of course, I wanted to keep a positive attitude and to assure the kids that it was going to be okay.

I had been in for surgery so many times myself that hospitals didn't really scare me. So it was not until I went up to see Joy that I realized how badly she was injured. The doctors had installed a metal halo—a circular steel brace screwed right into her head and connecting to her shoulders—to stabilize her neck. When I saw her like that, I think I finally realized what had happened.

At that minute, the doctor walked in and said, very matter-of-factly, "She will never walk again."

What? I could not believe it. Even if it was true that Joy was paralyzed, I could not believe the doctor could be so blunt. "Wait a minute," I said. "You guys have only had her here for an hour and a half, how can you say something like that? I mean, isn't there *some* kind of hope?" And the doctor said, "Well, I have been doing this a long time, so don't try to tell me how to do my job. Do you want me to give her false hope?" This was the old-school type of attitude toward the treatment for spinal cord injuries, before the recent advances in stem cell research that give hope to patients today.

I told the doctor, "Of course we want hope, even false hope." And Joy said to him, "You don't know me. How can you say that?" So the doctor said, "You want percentages? I'll give her a 3 percent chance of ever walking again." With that, Joy looked up at him and, with more courage and conviction than I have ever seen in my life, said, "I'll take that 3 percent chance. It's better than no chance."

I have never been prouder of someone in my entire life than I was of Joy at that moment. I felt like a giant weight had been lifted off my shoulders. Joy is a nurse and she knows a lot about medicine, so she was right to keep a positive mental attitude and to focus on that 3 percent chance instead of the alternative. Researchers have proven in recent years that a positive, hopeful mental outlook can have a great effect on the level and rate of a patient's recovery. In some cancer studies, for example, doctors have found that a patient's optimistic attitude can improve the outcome by 40 to 60 percent.

Needless to say, I was very pissed off at the doctor for his thoughtless bedside manner. In fact, I took the doctor aside and said, "What kind of asshole would say something like that to a patient who is obviously going through such mental gymnastics right now?" He just turned around and walked right out on me. I wanted to punch him right in the nose. I am sure that if Joy could have, *she* would have punched him right in the nose.

Not knowing what the rest of our lives held in store for us and for the children, I could not hold back the tears. I looked at my beautiful wife with that heavy metal halo screwed onto her head, and I didn't know what to think or how to feel. No one can prepare for the intense emotions caused by such a horrible event. I was terrified of our unknown future, and my emotions flooded over. At the same time, I was also enormously proud of how Joy was handling the situation.

That was probably the first time in my life that I was really scared to death. I was frightened for Joy, frightened for my children, and frightened for myself. What would Joy's quality of life be? Was she going to live? Was she really going to be paralyzed the rest of her life? It was just like someone had punched me in the stomach, like all the air had been knocked out of my body. I was just physically exhausted. For a guy that always has an answer for something, for the first time in my life, I had no answer. I didn't even know what questions to ask.

In his first inaugural address in 1933, at the depth of the Great Depression, Franklin D. Roosevelt is famous for reassuring the American people that "the only thing we have to fear is fear itself—nameless, unreasoning, unjustified terror which paralyzes needed efforts to convert retreat into advance." Well, for the first time in my life I fully understood the depth and meaning of that quote as I struggled to hold on to my wits. It was like I had fallen into some giant, dark hole in the universe, and I felt that I was never going to find my way out. It was so dark, I didn't know right from left or up from down. I got weak in the knees and felt sick to my stomach. And although I had no idea at the time, things were actually about to get much worse.

A lot of people called us when they heard the bad news. I suppose my kids got on the phones to cancel their evening activities, and the word spread quickly. Steve Palermo, a Major League Baseball umpire who had a spinal cord disability, came to the hospital to see us and offered to help us find good medical care in the Kansas City area. Steve recommended a surgeon and a group of physicians who had worked with Steve and with his foundation, The Steve Palermo Foundation for Spinal Cord Research. So on July 7, we moved Joy from St. Joseph's Hospital to the University of Kansas Medical Center.

At KU, they had to place more hardware in Joy's neck, but the surgeon screwed up majorly and accidentally ran three metal screws through the wall of her esophagus, putting holes in three different places. I guess doctors are only human and they make mistakes, but this was a very serious error that almost killed Joy and seriously delayed her potential recovery. After the procedure, bacteria simply invaded her body tissues through the holes they had punched in her esophagus every time she ate. While Joy was still recovering from the procedure in the ICU, her face puffed up like a balloon because of infection and related gases building up in her tissues from the wounds to her esophagus. On top of that, she was in intense pain and was not getting enough pain medication to alleviate it.

Joy wasn't getting any better, but after only two days in the ICU they decided to move her out anyway to a step-down unit. A day later, Joy said, "I don't belong here. I am going to die here. I need to be in the ICU. There is something seriously wrong here." So they went back and discovered that the doctor had punctured the esophagus in three places. They took Joy back to surgery, and now I was really pissed off. Joy's face was so badly swollen that she could hardly see, and to make things worse, no one seemed to be alarmed about this or to be doing anything about it. I was furious, and in my anger, I made a stupid comment to the doctor who was going to go in and fix her esophagus. I said, "You know, when I played in the NFL, and made a mistake, they put it up on the scoreboard: 'DOBLER—HOLDING.' Well, you doctors have got it made, don't you? When you make mistakes you just bury them, don't you?"

I realized afterward that it had been a pretty harsh thing to say, so I tried to do some backpedaling. I also decided to get Joy into a different hospital. But where should I take her? I felt I had already made a bad decision by having her moved to KU. Now I had to make another decision that may make the difference between life and death. I prayed for guidance.

The next day I figured that God must have heard my prayers, because Pat Rummerfield called me from St. Louis and said he would like me to meet Dr. John McDonald, the doctor who was working with none other than Christopher Reeve. Of course, I had known about Christopher Reeve's spinal cord injury and figured that he must have the best doctors, so after a long conversation with Pat, I bought a plane ticket to St. Louis the next day.

My old Cardinals teammate Keith Wortman picked me up at the airport and drove me to see Dr. McDonald, who is now the director of the International Center for Spinal Cord Injury at the Kennedy Krieger Institute, affiliated with the Johns Hopkins University Hospital in Baltimore, Maryland. At the time, he was working on stem cell research in St. Louis at Barnes-Jewish Hospital. Keith joined me during the discussion, as I thought he could give me an outside opinion without being emotionally involved.

Dr. McDonald had examined all of Joy's records and X-rays and gave us a very good presentation. More important, to my great relief, Dr. McDonald gave me hope and encouragement. He told me that he believed with the research they were doing, Joy had an excellent chance of walking again.

It was like I had died and gone to heaven. I was so excited to get back to Kansas City and tell Joy. Keith called Dan Dierdorf, and they started making arrangements to have Joy moved to St. Louis. My only reservation was that St. Louis was four hours away from our home, and I didn't want to be that far away from Joy. But both Dan and Keith assured me that between the two of them and their wives, all of Joy's needs would be met in St. Louis. Dan also made sure that a jet was available to take

Joy to St Louis. What great friends; without the support of Dan Dierdorf, Keith Wortman, Jim Hanifan, Dr. John McDonald, and his colleague, Dr. Cristina Sadowsky, Joy might have died.

After seven days at KU's Medical Center, we transferred Joy to the Barnes-Jewish Hospital in St. Louis where she stayed for the next 31 days. At Barnes, Joy was working with the team of Pat Rummerfield, Dr. McDonald, Dr. Sadowsky, and some other great physicians, several of whom are still working with her today. These are the folks who informed us about the potential of stem cell research. Meanwhile, I went back to Kansas City and was trying to take care of things at the office, but all I could really think about was Joy.

I was not getting much work done and I was just walking around like a zombie, so I went back to be with Joy in St. Louis, at times sleeping on the floor in the hospital room. So I was out of the office when things with the business were going to hell, and of course Joy couldn't work. I felt like I had been hit by a truck. We still had young children—Franco was in high school, Holli was in the eighth grade, and Stephen was in the sixth grade. Fortunately, my youngest sister, Casey, moved down to Kansas City to help me out with the kids. I couldn't have managed without her. While Joy was at Barnes for those 31 days, I spent almost two weeks of that time by her bedside watching over her while Casey took care of the kids.

At Barnes they had to remove all of the hardware from Joy's body to allow her esophagus to heal. She was being fed through tubes in her stomach, and she had to lie in bed without being moved for three weeks but without any hardware to immobilize her. The thing about spinal cord injuries is that the sooner you start rehabilitation, the better the chances are the patient will have at least a partial recovery. They say that every day of rehabilitation that you miss after the injury adds six months to your recovery process. Because Joy was injured for two days before the first surgery, then had to wait another four weeks to heal from the damage they had done to her esophagus, it was about six weeks before she could even start rehabilitation.

On August 14, 2001, we were able to move Joy to the rehab hospital across the street where Dr. McDonald and Dr. Sadowsky had their research labs. They put Joy in a private room that was connected to a living room suite, a kitchen, and an additional bedroom. No more sleeping on the floor for me. Joy spent nine months at their facility, and the family and I made a lot of trips to St. Louis to be near her.

Since we were going to be spending so much time in St. Louis, I figured it would be a good idea to open an office there. I hired Dan Dierdorf's daughter to run that facility; I felt if she needed some help, she could consult with Joy and it would be good for Joy to keep her mind occupied. Unfortunately, a month after we hired Dan's daughter, she was forced to have back surgery and could not work for months. So I had to close that office and get out of the leases. At that point, our company was really bleeding money. Basically, no one was minding the store when I was in St. Louis going through these difficult months with Joy.

That September I had been invited to play in the Aon Golf Tournament in Chicago with Pat Ryan, who was the chairman of the board of Aon and a minority owner of the Chicago Bears. I really couldn't afford time away from the office and Joy, but this was a charity golf tournament for a good cause and would get my mind off things for a couple days.

On September 11, 2001, the morning after the golf outing, I caught a flight from Chicago to St. Louis to spend the day with Joy. Fortunately I got an early flight that departed around 7:00 AM. When I walked into the rehab center around 9:00 AM, Joy told me to turn on the TV to see what had happened in New York City and Washington, D.C. Like the rest of the world, I had a hard time believing what I was seeing. I don't think anyone in America will ever forget that moment. Of course, all the flights were now grounded and people were stranded all over the country, so someone had to drive from Kansas City to pick me up.

Back in Kansas City, I went directly to the office to see the new guy I just hired to replace our CFO, but I was informed that he had disappeared about two hours after the attacks on the World Trade Center and the Pentagon. I found this somewhat strange. The staff had complained that this fellow was one brick short of a full load. He had told some of my staff that he usually takes jobs like this one, finds accounting errors, and has the owners put in jail. He said he had made himself millions of dollars in the process.

I figured that the staff members were a little paranoid, thinking that their jobs may be on the line, but I guess they were right about him. Three days later, on September 14, 2001, this guy returned to the office with a Marine-style haircut and informed me that he had been called up for duty and was being transferred to a military installation in Georgia *and* that they had made him a general *and* that he was going to be in charge of "Marshall Law in Kansas City." I brought him into my office and told him that I thought he should quit since it looked like he was going to be real busy. I think this guy belonged in a hospital for the very, very nervous.

Back in the office after a three-month absence, I realized that our situation was headed from bad to worse. I spent a lot of time firing managers, some of whom had been embezzling from us, and closing offices that were bleeding cash. As if I didn't have enough on my mind, that January the children decided to go visit Joy one weekend, and their car got rear-ended. I had to drop everything and go to St. Louis to get the car fixed and to pick up the kids.

Joy returned to continue her daily rehabilitation in Kansas City in May of 2002. The rehab facility in Kansas City could not compare to the facility in St. Louis, however. The facility in St. Louis was designed to treat spinal cord injuries and brain injuries with an emphasis on recovery and a cure through physical therapy, while the facility in Kansas City was just designed to help you adjust to being in a wheelchair. After three months, the insurance company said they were cutting Joy's coverage back from five days of rehabilitation per week to three days. The facility told her that she could take care of herself in a wheelchair and that she should go home, get used to being handicapped, and learn to live with it.

Refusing to accept defeat, in August of 2002 Joy switched to a facility in San Diego called Project Walk. Thankfully, Casey moved out to be with her. But the rehab center cost $6,000 per month, the apartment was $1,500, and Casey was paid $2,000 to cover her expenses. Add the cost of travel and prescriptions, and we were spending about $12,000 per month on Joy's care. Because of the second mortgage, our house payments were around $7,000 per month. Two private high schools, one catholic grade school, and college expenses for Erin were running another $3,000 per month. After adding in household expenses, insurance, and utilities, our total monthly expenses were now running around $25,000 per month.

There comes a time when you have choices to make, when you have to choose which bridge to cross and which bridge to burn. I needed to come up with the money for Joy's rehab. I had my own Rubicon to cross. I knew there would be some collateral damage, but sometimes you must sacrifice your own ideals for the good of others. In order to pay for all of this, I decided to start paying myself dividends out of the company; I had stopped paying myself a salary to cut costs a long time ago. I thought that I would be able to write this off as medical expenses at the end of the year.

With such a financial burden, I knew that this storm was growing and was quickly reaching the point of being out of control, but I had no idea how bad things would eventually become. I had made it through some tough times, but now I was spending most of my time trying to make ends meet and had even less time to manage the business. I had to sell our place in Copper Mountain, Colorado, cash in our 401(k), empty our savings accounts, sell the office building in Wichita, and refinance the office building in Kansas City. And it still wasn't enough to support our household, pay the children's school expenses, and finance Joy's rehab.

In March of 2003, Stephen was entering his last year of grade school and Joy wanted to coach the basketball team; she wanted to be there for him. Holli was also preparing for her confirmation, and Joy certainly wanted to be present for that. So Joy returned home from San Diego, this time without Casey to help her. Frankly, though, we just couldn't afford to keep them out there any longer. Since leaving San Diego, Joy has cut back on her rehabilitation therapy, partly because the costs are so high, and partly because she has really set her sights on finding a cure through stem cell research.

I, in turn, have learned how to do things that I never dreamed of doing now that I am one of Joy's primary caretakers. On most days, I help Joy get her day started. First, I get up around 6:00 AM to give her a pain pill and also take one for my own pain. Once Joy's pain pill kicks in around 7:00 AM, we can start moving her. The next task I have to perform is to help Joy take care of her bodily functions, which requires skilled and careful use of a catheter. This can take up to an hour at times, and learning how to do it properly was very challenging. After that I start working and stretching her legs, help her bathe, and finally help her get dressed and into her chair. At this point it is around 10:00 or 10:30 AM, and we both have breakfast. It's ironic, I guess, that before the accident we sometimes didn't get out of our pajamas until noon because we were so busy working. Now, on mornings when I have to help Joy (which is most mornings), I am lucky to make it to the office by 11:00 AM. In addition to the morning routine, there are several other household duties I have had to take over as well. With my own physical limitations, I am challenged, but I find myself with no other choice but to keep moving forward and to persevere through the difficulties. I work late in the office and go in early when I can.

For Holli's confirmation, each child had to write a letter to the bishop discussing why they wanted to be confirmed. The bishop read Holli's letter during the ceremony; it was about how her faith had helped her through the trouble our family was experiencing. That letter really got to me. For a big guy, I sure had been tearing up a lot over the last couple of years. In addition to just trying to keep from sinking in the stormy waters, I also tried to keep things in perspective; the most important things were Joy's health and the children's well-being. But, like my dad, I showed love by providing for my family, and I was becoming increasingly worried about my ability to do so. On the horizon, more trouble was brewing.

For some reason we seemed to be a convenient target for people who were incompetent, unethical, or just plain stupid. We were ripped off, robbed, and even sued by our own employees, whom we had always treated well. One of them, the mother-in-law of our incompetent CFO, had even secretly filed a false complaint for overtime with the labor board that I had to address. She then quit her job and sued me for age discrimination. This was a woman who could barely work at all and had made many costly mistakes, but Joy and I had kept her on for eight years out of loyalty and the goodness of our hearts. So much for kindness being repaid.

After barely avoiding a huge payroll catastrophe by using Joy's disability money to cover a $100,000 shortfall, I found out in June of 2003 that we had $1.2 million in accounts receivable...which had never been collected. I was fed up with that kind of bullshit, so I fired our CFO. In January of 2004, my key employee and office manager quit, taking off with 30 files of my private-duty patients to open her own agency with someone else. This woman was a single mother whose house I had helped furnish with couches and end tables. I guess now I know what it means when they say "no good deed goes unpunished."

It was getting impossible to pay attention to all the different plates we had spinning. Joy had a broken neck and was going through all this medical stuff; we were bleeding money, closing offices, and fighting a $10 million lawsuit and a $20,000 labor board complaint; we had $1.2 million in past-due accounts to collect; we had to pay unemployment compensation for the staff I fired; we were paying for Franco's tuition at Baker, Holli's private high school, and Stephen's private grade school; and Abby was starting college at KU.

Just when I thought the storm couldn't get any worse, it did. I soon found out that I was not allowed to write off the $115,000 in medical expenses for Joy because you can only write off medical expenses on earned income, not on dividends. I couldn't afford to take it as earned income because I would not have had enough money left after taxes to support Joy's care, so I ended up owing the IRS $45,000, which I did not have. We got on a payment plan with the IRS, but I had to close the Austin and Wichita offices and focused on collecting the $1.2 million dollars of accounts receivable.

In December of 2005, I learned I needed to have surgery on my ailing knee. I went in for my first knee replacement on my right knee, which at the time was the 11th knee surgery of my life. But the knee replacement was just the beginning; I needed 10 more surgeries over the next four years. My rehabilitation was going fairly well after the 2005 knee replacement, but in early January of 2006, all of a sudden I couldn't get out of bed.

I had been living downstairs because I didn't want Joy to be exposed to any possible infections I may have picked up in the hospital, and so I called my friend Steve Brown, a former football player at the University of Wyoming who happens to be a dentist, and I told him that I couldn't breathe and that my leg was killing me. He said I needed to get to the hospital and called Marty Gray, another former player from Wyoming who lived in St. Joseph, Missouri, to come and help my 16-year-old son Stephen get me to the hospital. Marty made it to my house in 45 minutes, and he and Stephen helped me into the van.

I was really having trouble breathing, and Stephen kept saying, "Dad, don't die, don't die." I was in the ER in a private room, and I heard the doctor talking to Joy and Marty. The doctor said if they had not gotten me to the hospital when they did, I would have been dead within two hours. They were talking softly, and so I shouted out, "Hey, my leg is hurt, but I am not deaf."

I owe my life to Steve and Marty for reacting so fast and helping Stephen to get me to the hospital. My boy Stephen really did a great job that day, too. He could have freaked out, but he rose to the occasion and really came through for me. I was very proud of Stephen that day, and I will never forget that those three people saved my life.

I had developed an infection in the artificial knee called MRSA. The surgeons had to wash out all the hardware, and then they put me on an antibiotic IV twice a day for six weeks. After six weeks they operated again and found out that I still had the MRSA, which meant another six weeks of IV therapy, twice a day, at $1,000 a day in medical expenses. At that point we had to have a nurse come to the house to take care of both me and Joy. The children also became our caretakers, having to do chores and errands and business-related tasks that Joy and I would normally handle. Six weeks later I went back in for another surgery and they removed the hardware in the knee and replaced it with spacers full of antibiotics, after which I was walking with a walker and had pick lines coming out of my arms. These pick lines got infected, so then I had to have one placed in my chest.

I soon realized, as Joy had in her own case right after the accident, that I might die if I didn't get out of Kansas City. Again I made a call to Dan Dierdorf and asked him to help me find a doctor. Once again Dan helped me out, and he found Dr. Doug McDonald in St. Louis. I was admitted to Barnes-Jewish Hospital, the same hospital where Joy had been a patient, and I was there for over a month fighting the infections. In fact, they removed everything and just left the knee open for one week. While working to get the MRSA cleaned up in the right knee, the doctors found out that the hardware in my left knee had failed, the bones were damaged, and I would need that knee replaced—for the third time. So I had the pleasure of knowing that once my right knee had fully recovered, I would need to return to the hospital and start all over with my left knee.

Around this time, we found out that a nurse who had been working in our home had helped herself to my credit cards, Joy's wedding ring, some cash, and some of the kids' clothing. She ran up $30,000 on my credit cards within a two-month period. We also found out that someone had written about $15,000 in forged checks from our account. We closed that account, and someone later transferred $100,000 out of the closed account. At that point, the bank was investigating us.

I am not the type of person to throw in the towel, but I just didn't see how I could keep all these plates spinning, so I told Joy that we might have to file for bankruptcy. We went to see this bankruptcy attorney, and while I was in the waiting room to meet with the attorneys I picked up the new issue of *Inc.* magazine. Well, guess who was on the cover as the "Entrepreneur of the Year"? It was Joy's old boyfriend—the same guy who fired her. He had taken his company public and was doing very well. And here I was, getting ready to talk to a bankruptcy attorney.

I thought, *Boy, did Joy make a big mistake picking me over him.* But it turned out that it was just what I needed, because I thought to myself, *Fuck it. If he can do it, then so can I.* I decided to just go back and keep fighting. In reality the cards were really stacked against me. But that was nothing new. They had been stacked against me for a long time. I really didn't know how I was going to get out of the hole we were in, but I was not done fighting. I was going to hold onto the anchor all the way to the bottom of the ocean before I would quit.

Unfortunately, it seems that sometimes the color of justice in America is green; in other words, if you have enough money you can make the law read any way you want it. I could have fought our former employee and won against her frivolous suit, but it would have cost me $80,000 and a lot of energy, and all I would have won was the right to say "I was right and you were wrong." In the end, the best option was to write her a check for $25,000 to make her go away. A friend of mine once said, "Don't let your pride get in the way of your pocket book." To this day I am still pissed about having to give in and write that check, but I needed the time to get back to the other plates I had spinning. It was time to move on. I had to focus on Joy's health and my health, while still trying to keep the business going.

My 20-year struggle with the National Football League Players Association (NFLPA) has been especially taxing during the last 10 years, as well. When I retired from the NFL in 1981, I received no information at all from them in regard to the benefits I was entitled to after 10 years in the league. I never thought that I would spend two decades fighting with the NFLPA to gain disability benefits from the very union that I supported and was a member of all those years. I never dreamed that the NFL itself would turn its back on me.

The saddest thing is that I am not alone in this situation; thousands of former NFL players—including many of the greatest names in the sport— are now disabled as a result of the injuries they suffered during their playing days, and their union, the NFLPA, has completely turned its back on these guys. Many former players often find themselves financially destitute and with no way to care for their debilitating health issues, many of which don't start to show up until 10 or 15 years after playing their last down. It's a huge issue with often tragic consequences for many of the guys who have provided countless hours of entertainment to the people all across the nation on Sunday afternoons (and Monday, Thursday, and even Saturday nights) and whose athletic skills and physical sacrifices have enabled the NFL to become the multi-billion dollar industry that it is today.

My knees had really started giving me problems soon after I retired, so I called a lawyer to see what benefits the NFLPA could offer me. I met with Gerry Spence, who at that time was one of the premier trial lawyers in the United States. Gerry had just won the Silkwood case, the story about radiation exposure at a nuclear power plant that was eventually made into a blockbuster movie. Even with his famous name, Gerry could not get through to talk to anyone in the NFLPA. He said, "Let me tell you about unions, Conrad. They are not going to do anything for you once you are no longer a part of the union."

I could not believe that. I said he must have been mistaken. After all, I had played side by side with these guys for a decade; I had been on strike with these guys in the 1970s and they all knew me. Surely these same guys, who were now running the NFLPA, would be willing to help me. But guess what? After 20 years, I am still fighting to gain disability support from the NFLPA. The fight has drained me of my financial resources, my time, and my energy, and it has caused me much mental, emotional, and psychological anguish. I never expected this cruel and unusual punishment and callous disregard for the well-being of former NFL players from the NFL and NFLPA.

Here I was, walking around on crutches after a surgery performed to clean up the junk floating around in my knee. My knees were just bone on bone, and I was on heavy doses of Percocet to survive the excruciating pain. I had no choice. I was taking them by the handful. I knew that every time I moved, I was causing more damage to the knee joint, and the drugs were also really screwing with my head. My energy levels, mental abilities, and emotions were all over the place. It was so bad that when I would come down off the medication, the pain would come back, and I would slide into an emotional depression prone to angry outbursts. I was barely able to hold myself together.

Hell, at times I was a complete, raving idiot. "Goddamn it, answer that damn phone!" I would snap. "Dad, it only rang once," one of the kids would say. Something as insignificant as not being able to find the remote control for the TV was getting me highly agitated, and I became somewhat tyrannical with my children, my wife, and anyone else within earshot. I think the kids noticed my strange behavior before Joy did, and I would hear them say to each other anxiously, "Hey, go get Daddy's medicine." They'd come over to me and say, "Here Dad, take one of these." And my daughter would be there with a glass of water: "Here's some water to take it down, Daddy."

One time I yelled, "Where are my goddamn keys?" The kids jumped up and ran around the house looking for them. I found them myself, got in the car, put my crutches in, and then I realized I forgot my coat. When I went back inside to get it, I found my daughter hiding in the closet. I yelled, "What the hell are you doing in the closet?" She told me she was looking for my car keys. Then it dawned on me that she had been hiding in there—hiding from *me*—until I left the house. Instead of realizing that I had terrified the poor girl, I went off on her about hiding in the closet and not looking for the keys like everyone else. I was pretty hard on everyone close to me, even the people I care about the most. I was so out of my head with the pain that I have no idea how Joy or the kids perceived my condition.

All they knew was that if they could get more pills in me, then everything would be okay until I went to bed or until the pills started to wear off. I really felt everything was going along just fine. I was drinking alcohol and I also smoked some weed to help me deal with the pain and the stress. That probably only made it worse in the long run. During that period, the entire household was walking around as if the floor were made of eggshells, afraid that I could go off at any minute. I was behaving like a total asshole; everything just set me off. I wasn't feeling good. I couldn't work. I was pissed off and frustrated.

At one point I was classified by the NFLPA's own doctor as "75 percent disabled." Yet, the NFL disability board tabled my application for disability for months. While I was waiting for them to review my case, I was taking massive amounts of narcotic medication to deal with the unimaginable pain I suffered. After three months of indecision, the NFLPA review board (which, by the way, does not even include a single medical doctor) decided to table their discussion "until their next meeting." That meeting was another six months away.

The NFL and NFLPA have given me virtually no help at all. The NFLPA stonewalled me and just kept sending me paperwork and more paperwork. I got nothing but the runaround. Instead of helping me, they delayed, time and again, the disability application process for so many months while they were "doctor shopping" me around for a medical opinion they wanted to agree with. At one point they even hired an incompetent lawyer to sue the New Orleans Saints for earnings owed to me when I was injured; the thing is, the Saints had paid me when I was injured. The NFLPA delayed the application process for so long that the eligibility period for disability coverage had finally expired, a fact they were happy to point out to me. I have recently found out that I can file for workers' compensation, and I am in the process of doing so. Outrageously, I am not alone in this situation. My experience is similar to the plight of just about every former player who files for disability.

I knew I needed help with the medication and the pain, and of course the children and Joy felt that they couldn't live with me like that anymore. So without any help or support from the NFLPA, I decided for the good of the family and myself that I needed to get my left knee replaced. It was either get it replaced or I would likely end up committing suicide from the pain and effects of the drugs. I arranged to have the knee replaced, and I figured I would have to come up with the $10,000 deductible. I figured that I would get it back when the NFLPA approved my disability application. This surgery cost me $30,000, and after 20 years, I am still waiting for the NFLPA to pay its first penny.

I could go on and on at length describing my horrible odyssey and battle with the NFLPA. I could talk about the numerous delays, the denied applications, the catch-22s, the bureaucratic hocus-pocus, the various doctors' opinions, the unanswered requests for help, and the incompetence, negligence, and callousness of an organization that manages a $1.2 billion fund but has shirked its legal responsibility to address the dire issues faced by the thousands of former NFL players on whose backs today's NFL was built. But there are not enough pages in this book (or in *War and Peace* for that matter) to do so. Maybe that should be the subject of my next book.

The bottom line is that the NFLPA just threw me under the bus, along with the large majority of retired players who are suffering and are denied any disability benefits. After all the strikes I joined in solidarity with my union brothers, and after all the times I put my job on the line to support the union's goals, the same union has told me to just go off and find a hole to die in. As far as retired players go, the NFLPA's strategy seems to be, "Delay, deny, and hope they die." Well I am still alive, and I will continue this fight for as long as I can to see that justice is served.

The cards are stacked against any retired player who needs to go before the disability board. The NFLPA representatives for the players are Tom Condon, who is one of the top player agents in the NFL; Jeff Van Note, who does the radio broadcast for the Atlanta Falcons; and former NFL player Dave Duerson. All three of these men have connections with the NFL owners on the other side of the table. If any of them disagreed with the owners, they could lose their jobs and their incomes. Talk about a conflict of interest! A first grader could see this. I remember having dinner one night with Tom Condon, and he told me, "Sure, you can sue the disability board of the NFLPA, but we never lose." I found that so arrogant and disgusting. Instead of bragging about how powerful the NFLPA is, Condon should have been working with me to help me get my claim approved. I told him that, and he just looked at me and coldly said, "That's the way it is. Live with it."

If my family and I had not received such incredibly generous help and support from people outside of football—completely unsolicited assistance—I don't know how we would have made it this far. Without organizations like Mike Ditka's Gridiron Greats Assistance Fund, along with other organizations and individuals who have selflessly stepped forward to help out, my family and I would probably be living in a box somewhere. The late Gene Upshaw once said that he and the NFLPA did not represent retired players. He also said that he could have the best product in the world, but if you can't sell it, "what good is it?" I say, if you have the best product and you can't sell it, then you need to get a better salesman.

I know I am on the right side of this issue, and I will continue to battle the NFLPA until I am able to bring about the necessary changes to the system. I will continue to fight the good fight for all retired players until their pensions are increased to where the Major League Baseball players' pension is and until disability assistance is granted to those who need it. It's simply the right thing to do. Like my dad said of his WWII experiences, sometime circumstances place you in the middle of a situation, and you have to do the right thing, for yourself and for your fellow man. And so I call upon the NFL and the NFLPA to step up and address this issue; it is time for them to do the right thing. The NFL's "dirtiest player" hates to lose, and I've lost some battles but am committed to winning this war.

So we find ourselves today still right in the middle of the perfect storm; still trying to keep things afloat; still trying to get what we feel we deserve; fighting for justice for ourselves, the NFL players who need relief, and for those 1 million people in this country with spinal cord injuries for whom the promising advances of stem cell science offer so much hope for the future. (I applaud the Obama administration for its position on the subject.) We will always remain very grateful for the love and support of those who have seen our plight and the plight of others in need and who have thrown us a lifeline to help keep us afloat, to enable us to fight for our health, for justice, and for a good quality of life. We will continue to fight and to give back to others who need help.

8

RANDOM ACTS OF KINDNESS: PAYING IT FORWARD

"For someone who had been labeled
'pro football's dirtiest player,'
I must have done something right
for so many people to have come forward
with these random acts of kindness."

As a society and as individuals, we must realize that we are not really separate from each other, that our individuality is just an illusion—like a persona. In truth, we are all part of the same universe, and we have an obligation and a duty to give back to society. Every living organism exists for a purpose. Our purpose in life is to give back to the world we live in and to make it a better place, not only for ourselves, but for all people. My family and I have come to know many amazing individuals who truly understand this concept. Joy and I have always believed in and understood the importance of giving back, no matter what circumstances we may find ourselves in. But in recent years we have found ourselves the recipients of extraordinary support from family and friends. There are so many people who have helped me and my family, people who continue to give their time and their resources to help others in need. We have been touched, uplifted, and encouraged by the kindness and compassion of these people. Because of this, I think we have developed a deeper understanding of the importance of giving back any way we can and of the impact that random acts of kindness can have on a life, a heart, and a soul.

I don't know how Joy and I could have made it this far since 2001 without the incredible help we have received from people who have learned what I believe is a very important lesson: that giving of yourself in whatever way possible makes the world a better place for all of us, and that "living is giving." We may have gone from the "Greatest Generation" to the "Me Generation," but so many people have come to our assistance—including people we had known closely for years, neighbors, classmates of our children, the church community, and total strangers—that I am encouraged for the future of America. I only wish it was possible to name everyone who has helped us in these few pages.

Joy and I have always been involved in community and charitable activities. As a former NFL player, I have always participated in benefits and charities, flying around the country for golf events and fund-raisers and giving of my time to help others. I even once auctioned off my services as a chef. (Well, I *am* a damn good gourmet chef!) Joy also has a long history of volunteering in community activities, giving money, time, and whatever else she could for all sorts of causes. Now, we are not ones who volunteer expecting something in return. We enjoy doing it because we just feel it is the right thing to do and makes the world a better place. As a result of our participation in community activities, we have been blessed to meet some great people and have made some great friends. Well, it sure didn't take long for those friends to step up as soon as the word got out that Joy Dobler had been paralyzed by a spinal cord injury. The outpouring of love and support we received was really overwhelming!

At first it was difficult to accept because I have always been helping people, not the other way around. I was a former NFL Pro Bowl player, the guy who always stepped up to help out. Being on the receiving end for me was both embarrassing and humbling; it was even damaging to my ego. But it did help me put into perspective just how difficult it had to be for others to ask for or to accept help. It also made Joy and I realize for the first time the type of impact the things we had done over the years had on people and how important that had been to the people we helped. We gained a better appreciation and firsthand knowledge of what even the smallest act of kindness can do and the effect that it can have on the human spirit.

It is very difficult to express in words the gratitude that Joy and I feel to those who have reached out to help. The Dobler family did not go hungry during the time after Joy's accident. In fact, we had so many people cooking food and bringing it to our house that I had to start calling people and asking them to drop food off at the homeless shelters because we had no more space in the refrigerator! We thanked them, and Joy and I really appreciated all their concern.

The kids at school set up a program called "Pennies for a Prayer for Joy Dobler," where the kids would put pennies into a giant water bottle to give to Joy. Well, they filled two of them up, and they were so heavy I had to get someone to help me load them into my car. In all I think I cashed them in for around $600; that is 60,000 pennies! My car looked like a lowrider when I went to the bank. But it was a great thing and a beautiful effort on the part of those children.

Michael Garozzo, who owns three Italian restaurants in Kansas City and also wore my number when he played football in high school, found out about Joy's accident the day it happened, and he immediately called his good friend Steve Palermo. Steve was a baseball umpire who had been shot in the back while trying to stop a thief from stealing a girl's purse, and he had suffered a spinal cord injury as a result. Michael asked Steve to reach out to us, and Steve came to the hospital the very same day that Joy was injured and spent time with her in the ICU, telling her not to give up hope, that he had been in the same position and worked hard to recover. Steve's giving of his time and knowledge provided us great support and comfort. He gave us something that nobody could give us, something that money could not buy: Steve gave us hope. It is amazing the kind of impact something as simple as giving your time can have. Joy and I both appreciated Steve's effort, and we have remained friends to this day. We continue to help support each other's foundations for spinal cord injury research.

Michael Garozzo also knew that our medical bills would be enormous, so he asked our permission to organize a fund-raiser with his friend and ours, Keith Connell. Keith is one of the largest vegetable wholesalers throughout Missouri and Kansas. He was also a member of our church, and we were frequent golfing partners before my knees got so bad that I could no longer play golf. Michael and Keith sent out invitations to a $500-per-person event to raise money for Joy. They even hit up their vendors for donations. Well, the dinner party was a grand success. Even people who couldn't make it to the event bought tickets, including Dan Dierdorf, Jim Hanifan, and Dick Butkus, among others. Larry Stewart, who has since passed away, also came by and donated $1,000. Larry had made the national news as "the Secret Santa," going around and passing out $100 bills at Christmas. Carl Peterson of the Chiefs also came by, and Marty Schottenheimer's wife also stopped by with a check. The event raised more than $50,000 to put toward Joy's medical bills, and this helped get Joy into an advanced experimental rehabilitation program in San Diego. This money was used for Joy's rehabilitation, which in turn gave her optimism and reinforced her determination.

When the chips were down, I really started to understand the true meaning of the word *friend*. So many people showed their kindness and support that at one point I spent three straight days writing thank-you notes. Some of these people I knew well, and some I had never met before in my entire life. A simple "thank you" didn't seem like enough, but it was the only thing I had to offer. It did make me realize that I would have a responsibility to pass this gift of kindness along in the future to others who might need help. I now know how important it is to "pay it forward." Being able to share your wealth is great, but giving time is so much more important than money. I will always give of my time for the rest of my life, not just because of the many people who have donated their time to Joy and me and our family but because giving of yourself is the greatest gift any person has to offer.

Dan Dierdorf has been there for me and my family every step of the way. Dan is more than a friend; he is my brother. We've been in the trenches together. We fought side by side in the NFL. That's the thing about offensive linemen: we are trained to work as a team and not let the other guy down. We share a special bond. I don't want to compare what we did on the football field with a real war because the courage and training our men and women display in combat is so much greater as they risk their lives day in and day out for the deepest principles. Their lives are on the line, and all we had on the line as football players was our pride. But the bond we have as offensive linemen has got to be similar to the bond our soldiers experience in their training. Dan was always there for me in the NFL, like a combat buddy, and since 2001 he has given my family and me a lot of support, either directly or by making sure that all of our needs were met by other teammates while we were in St. Louis. Dan said to me, "Whatever you need, Conrad. Don't worry, if you gotta go home to the kids and stuff, I'm here. Whatever Joy needs, we'll make sure she gets it. Don't worry about a thing."

Dan wasn't the only one to step up and help. Keith Wortman, Jim Otis, Terry Miller, and a lot of my other teammates helped us when we were in St. Louis. They were all there to lend a tremendous amount of support. I think there is a vast difference between playing football and other professional sports, because I don't think you find those kinds of bonds in other places. In the football community, people just come together when someone's having a rough time. So many friends were there to lend their moral, financial, and physical support: "Need a place to stay? Stay at my house. Don't worry about it. Need to borrow a car? Here are the keys. Don't worry about it. Need someone to pick you up at the airport? We'll come get you."

The support from the entire St. Louis community was overwhelming. It was just an outpouring of love and support for me and my family. Most of these people didn't even know Joy. But thanks to Dan and these other great people, I knew whenever I left St. Louis to go back home that I was only a phone call away from having someone at Joy's bedside, taking care of whatever she needed. That was comforting to me and it made me feel really, really good. Joy was probably in better hands in St. Louis than she would've been with me trying to take care of the children, running back and forth and stuff. Without the support of all these people, Joy might have died.

Because of all the medical expenses, I had fallen behind on our house payments. As a result, the home where our kids had grown up was repossessed, and I needed some help with remodeling the new house to make it accessible for Joy. The only reason I was even able to buy a new house at all was because of the help of some of my banking friends, including Pat Fortman of Labette Bank.

Chuck Peters, another friend and golfing buddy, owns a large construction company, Peters and Associates, and he brought an entire crew over to redo the new house to make it more accessible for Joy. We had iron workers, painters, tile people, and carpenters all working on order from Chuck. I didn't receive one single bill. I asked Chuck how much I owed him, and he told me, "You don't pay your friends for helping you out."

Even my good friend Jerry Clinton, who was the local Budweiser distributor in St. Louis, a noted philanthropist, and a cancer survivor himself, generously helped support us. That in spite of the fact that I had been a spokesperson for Miller Lite! Thankfully, Jerry was willing to "cross enemy lines" to help out some good friends in their support of spinal cord research.

I was starting to understand what the Beatles meant when they sang, "I get by with a little help from my friends." Of course, your friends are your friends, and your family is your family; who else is going to come to your aid when you need help? Well, I was soon to learn that there are a lot of very kind and compassionate people out there who are ready and willing to help out anyone—even complete strangers—who might be in need. Sometime in 2003 or 2004, after Joy had returned from San Diego, our story was picked up and featured on HBO's *Real Sports with Bryant Gumbel*. They sent a camera crew over to the house, and they shot footage of me carrying Joy down the stairs and working on her stretching down in the weight room. David Humm, a good friend of mine and a former quarterback with the Bills who is now in a wheelchair himself, called me and said, "Conrad, what are you doing carrying your wife down the stairs? You can't even walk down the stairs yourself. What are you, an idiot?"

I really opened up about our situation on that show. I guess you could say I bared my soul. It's was kind of like a Barbara Walters interview. You know how she tries to ask questions that make people cry? Well, at the time my daughter Holli was really excelling in high school, graduating with honors. All my other children had been able to attend the college of their choice, but now I was so financially stressed that I had no means of sending Holli to college, and that really broke my heart. I told the cameras, "You know, what's really sad is my daughter is more deserving than anyone to pick any college she wants to go to, and now I can't afford to send her to college." As I said this, I started to tear up a little bit. I almost started to cry, and I said, "She's been accepted at many great colleges and she really deserves to go, but I can't afford to send her to any of them."

That night there were a couple of guys who were watching the show: a pro golfer by the name of Phil Mickelson and his friend and attorney Glenn Cohen. What they saw motivated them into one amazing act of kindness. Phil and Glenn immediately got on the phone with each other and decided to help my family out. "Do whatever it takes to help out," Phil had told Glenn. I did not know Glenn or Phil. I had never met or spoken to either of them, and then one day the phone rang. Glenn told me, "Phil Mickelson would like to help you. He would like to put Holli through college and give her the opportunity to go to whatever university she wants." Now I know it's hard to believe, but for one of the few times in my life, I was almost speechless. I was really shocked. I started to look for the right words while trying to hold on to my pride. I did not know what to say. I was a pro athlete who was being offered help from another pro athlete who was a *complete stranger* to me. Of course, I knew who Phil

Mickelson was, but I had never even met the guy. I wanted to say, "Thanks for the offer, but I don't really need the help." But in reality, I did need the help, and it was my daughter's future hanging in the balance. Thinking of Holli's opportunity enabled me to swallow my pride. I asked Glenn, "Why is Phil doing this?" Glenn said, "Don't worry about it. Phil's doing it because he can. He has a foundation set up for youth education programs." I said, "Well, what does Phil want from us?" Glenn said, "Nothing, and he'd appreciate it if you didn't tell anyone about it either." I said, "Well I just don't think 'thank you' is adequate." He said, "That's fine. Thank you is all you need to say." There's got to be something better than just thank you, but in the final analysis, sometimes that's all you can say.

So we kept it quiet for about a year. Then the press got a hold of it, and they started bugging Glenn and Phil. I wasn't saying anything, but they were still bugging me, Joy, and even Holli. Finally, Phil just decided to invite us to the Memorial Tournament in Ohio so we could make a formal announcement together; that way at least everyone would have the story straight.

Joy, Holli, and I went to lunch with Phil, his wife Amy, and Glenn, and that was when I met them for the first time. They are all really nice, and Phil acted like he was more excited about meeting me than I was about meeting him. He was calling me "Mr. Dobler," which made me look over my shoulder to see if my dad was standing behind me. Phil was just the nicest and most humble guy I have ever met, and while I knew that I was in the presence of golf greatness, I quickly learned that I was in the presence of a great man and a very classy guy.

So we had lunch and we talked a lot. Then we went into the press event. There were probably 50 to 75 press people there, and we answered numerous questions. There were also a bunch of one-on-one interviews; everyone wanted a sound bite. A lot of it had to do with the NFLPA and with Phil. At one point, one reporter asked my daughter, "How would you describe what Phil did?" Holli gave them the quote of the day when she replied, "There's only one way to describe it, and that's a random act of kindness. He didn't know me; he didn't know my dad; he didn't know anything about us. But he just knew that he had the ability to do something to help and did it with no questions asked and for nothing in return."

The most amazing part about that whole story—and this may sound arrogant, but I'm sure most parents feel the same way—is that I felt they couldn't have picked a better person to help than my daughter Holli. She took the opportunity Phil gave her and busted her ass, graduating summa cum laude from Miami (Ohio) in May of 2009, and doing it in four years with a major in English and a double minor in Spanish and linguistics. Holli also worked while she was going to college as a tutor for underclassmen.

As if funding Holli's education wasn't enough, Glenn and Phil knew that I had a son who was going into his senior year in high school. During Holli's senior year in college, Glenn called and said that Phil would be more than happy to also provide for Stephen's college tuition should we need the help. Well, we did, and once again Phil stepped up and is now putting my son Stephen through KU, where he is studying sports management. Hey, you never know; maybe someday Stephen will run the NFLPA and straighten that group out.

Phil's dad had served in the military just as mine did, and Glenn had also served in the armed forces. They had established a charity organization called Birdies for the Brave that supports the Special Operations Warrior Foundation, which helps raise college scholarships for the children of special ops soldiers who are lost in battle. Phil and Glenn are also involved with another organization called Homes for Our Troops that provides adapted housing for disabled veterans.

Phil and Glenn spent months looking at about 60 different charities before deciding to align with the Special Operations Warrior Foundation and Homes for Our Troops. Glenn once said, "Phil's visibility and his kindness and his philanthropy go through the ceiling. We do a lot of things for charity anonymously that people never know of; he will talk about Birdies for the Brave, and how wonderful it is, but he does not want to be the star. He does not want to be the focus. He gets involved because he understands that his name and face raise awareness." Phil funds a lot of charities, but the most important thing he gives is himself; his name brings awareness of these causes to millions. I can see why Phil has been nicknamed "the People's Choice."

In appreciation of Phil's support for my children's education, I thought it would be a nice gesture to give each of Phil's daughters a symbolic gift. I happened to own a set of antique gold French coins called "Lucky Gold Angel" coins. These are French 20 Franc gold coins with an angel stamped on them that were minted between 1871 and 1898 and are made of almost pure gold. There are many legends of good luck associated with the coins. For example, the coins' designer was next in line for the guillotine during the French Revolution when a bolt of lightning struck nearby and his life was spared. Ever since, the Gold Angel has been considered a lucky coin. Apparently, Napoleon Bonaparte carried a Gold Angel in his pocket for good luck, but he lost it the day before his crushing defeat at Waterloo. I gave these coins to Phil, one for each of his daughters to have (I also gave one to each one of my own daughters when they were going away to college). I told Phil, "Please give these to your daughters, and make sure that they have them so that there'll always be an angel by their side." I also gave Phil a rare, misprinted 50¢ piece; it was stamped heads on both sides. I think Phil has used that one as a ball marker. Anyway, I have learned that angels really do exist, and one of them is named Phil Mickelson. I hope that those of you who are reading this will pay it forward and step up to support one of Phil and Glenn's many great causes.

Another person who tuned into that HBO special was Jennifer Smith, who is the cofounder and was, at that time, the executive director of the Gridiron Greats Assistance Fund. The organization was founded by Jerry Kramer and was set up to provide social and medical services and financial aid to retired NFL players in crises. The organization's other mission is raising awareness about the issues faced by so many retired players and the lack of assistance provided by the NFL and the NFLPA. Many players have no health benefits at all and lack the financial ability to deal with health issues caused by injuries sustained while playing in the NFL.

Jennifer talked to us about the chance to help spread the Gridiron Greats message and to also see if she or the organization could assist us. We were more than happy for the opportunity to help out. At that time, I think pride kept most players from speaking out about their disabilities or their lack of financial means. Jennifer brought to our attention how many former players were dealing with these serious issues. Joy and I immediately knew that this was way bigger than our own situation. Jennifer asked us if we would be willing to help to raise awareness of the plight of so many retired NFL players by sharing our story and by being very public about our own fight to gain my disability benefits and support from the NFLPA.

We quickly agreed, and I said there were probably a lot of players and families that were a lot worse off than we were. I also told her that I had just received a call and that somebody wanted to donate $1,000 to us, but I had told them to give it to the Gridiron Greats. I really respect their cause and wanted to help. She seemed shocked that we did that, since she had been in our house all day and saw the challenges we faced. Today, Jennifer will tell you that it was at that point that she gained a deeper understanding of what "paying it forward" was really all about.

The *Real Sports* episode also touched the heart of Gene Bicknell, another fellow who helped out a lot. Gene used to own more than 700 Pizza Hut restaurants nationally and once ran for governor of Kansas. He was on vacation in Europe when he heard about Joy's injury. One day I received a letter from his son Marty, who was managing Gene's investment fund. In the letter, Marty said his dad had seen the piece on HBO in Europe, he wanted to help Joy and me, and that he had included a check.

When I first looked at the envelope with the return name of Mariner Wealth Advisors, I had assumed that it was from some stock broker trying to sell me something. I almost dumped it in the trash until I noticed that my name had been written by hand and wasn't on some printed-out label. I was really surprised to read Marty's letter, and while I was reading it the check had slipped out onto the floor. I was bending over in my chair to retrieve the check and noticed an amount. I thought it was for $2,000. I found my glasses, and that's when I saw the other zero: Gene's check was for $20,000. Boy, did I have a tough time putting into words how generous that was. It was a difficult task writing Gene a thank-you note because all I ever did for him was play in his charity golf tournaments when he asked me to.

The support we received then and still get today is endless. There are so many people out there, people like Paul Somerville and his late wife, Kathy, down in Houston. Paul has contributed several thousands of dollars to my wife's foundation and to spinal cord research. I had the opportunity to work with Kathy, who was sick with cancer at the time and who passed away about a year later. When I was in Houston, I would go to their house and visit with Kathy and cook dinner for them. Then there are Joy's friends, who come over to the house and pull the weeds, plant flowers, and volunteer to do all of the gardening for us. They do it every year. Then there are the ladies who come over and decorate our house for Christmas every season. These good friends of Joy's have nicknamed themselves "the Sod Sisters" and "the Christmas Elves," respectively. Ironically, one of the wonderful ladies in the group is Ginny Condon, Tom Condon's ex-wife; yes, that's the same Tom Condon who sits on the NFLPA disability board and who has denied me disability coverage for the last 30 years. (At least someone in that family knows how to do the right thing.)

Being on the receiving end of good will and kindness, while humbling, is very inspirational. Joy and I now take it upon ourselves to give back more than ever; Joy works to advance spinal cord science and stem cell research, while I am fighting for the plight of retired NFL players, helping Joy with her efforts for Kennedy Krieger, and volunteering my time at many special events around the country for a wide variety of important causes—including Caring for Kids and Food for the Homeless—and donating memorabilia to a variety of charities throughout the country. I feel as though my family and I have a giant responsibility to pay it forward. We have all heard the saying, "To whom much is given, much is asked." We have to try to give back any way we can. I may not be able to give away much money, but time I can give abundantly. Time is more important than money, because you can replace money; you can't replace time.

For someone who had been labeled "pro football's dirtiest player," I must have done something right for so many people to have come forward with these random acts of kindness. I think people have a tough time calling their friends when they need help, but true friends get pissed off if you need help and you *don't* call them. There is no loss of pride in accepting help from friends, and it is our friendships that enable us to persevere through life's most difficult challenges. People will really surprise you when you least expect it. Good friends are a real blessing in life and are one of life's great rewards.

My family has been through some very traumatic events over the last eight years. I get down at times, and then I remember the men and women fighting in places like Iraq and Afghanistan. This keeps me focused on what is important in life. When you have family and friends who are willing to support and help you, it is difficult to dwell on one's misfortunes. Of course it would be nice to also have your health, but with time and resources Joy and I are hopeful we can each recover.

Because of the love and generosity of the many people I have mentioned here, along with the many others I have not, I have become a better person. Joy and I have raised over $1.5 million in private donations for spinal cord science and stem cell research, and we have been able to send some high school and college kids with spinal cord injuries to

Kennedy Krieger Institute to be examined by the leading research scientists, giving many of those patients hope for a cure. The wonderfully generous people who have helped us have set the bar high for the rest of us. My hope is that the stories I have written about here will inspire every reader to perform random acts of kindness whenever they see an opportunity to help others in need and to continue to pay it forward.

9

DOING THE RIGHT THING

"I have always fought hard
for victory.
I am still fighting,
and I am just going to
keep on fighting."

A wise philosopher once said, "Of all the people you will know in a lifetime, you are the only one you will never leave nor lose." At this stage in my life, I have come to learn that all of the answers to the questions you face in life can be found inside of you. All the solutions to all the problems you have ever and will ever face are in you, too. The way I see it, life is a journey made up of a series of choices; we all make good choices and bad choices, but what's most important is learning from those choices.

Now, I am no angel. (I know that's hard to believe, but it's true.) I've made every mistake or bad choice that one person can make in a lifetime. I've had my share of ups and downs. I've been married twice. I have six children. I've been cut, traded, fired, and bankrupt. I've played in the NFL, written two books, hosted my own sports radio talk show, worked in the booth for both NFL and college football games, performed in numerous Miller Lite commercials, and did a Bic razor commercial. I've been on the cover of *Sports Illustrated*, had articles written about me in most national newspapers and magazines, and was a guest on most major sports TV and radio shows. I've had the opportunity to travel to many extraordinary places, such as Israel, Guam, Japan, Europe, and South America, all in first class, and I also have arguably the most famous knees in the world. I also serve on many charitable boards.

I've buried a sister, my father, and my father-in-law. I've got an 88-year-old mother who is happy in her own world. I have a mother-in-law who can't stand me, a sister who won the lottery but is still unhappy, and a rich brother who is a recovering alcoholic. My eldest son took 12 years to complete college and has a great marriage to his second wife. I've got a daughter with a pierced tongue and a tattoo that has a great husband and two beautiful children, and I have another daughter who runs a charitable organization in two states. I have a son who runs a company with his mother and doesn't share any information with me, a daughter that graduated from college with honors in 2009 and plans to attend law school, and a son who is a sophomore in college. My wife and I are business owners who are struggling during these economic times, and she is working harder than ever to overcome her injury and is striving with determination to one day walk again.

Maybe we have some giant challenges. But are we that different from the average American family? I can relate to each and every one of you reading this book, because I've been there and done that. Just because I am a former NFL player does not mean that my family and I don't face our share of very serious challenges. Too often we read books or listen to speakers who have lived a seemingly charmed life, and we listen or read with a certain degree of skepticism. Let me assure you, while I have surely had great opportunities, I have worked my ass off to capitalize on them and to learn from my mistakes as well.

I am you, each and every one of you. I am not a member of the silver spoon club. I was not born under a lucky star. I have experienced the good, the bad, and the ugly throughout my 58 years, sometimes because of my own doing. I have traveled many roads and I am still pursuing my dreams and building on my personal and business growth. I am not politically correct in my language nor am I politically correct in my life; I am who I am, and what you see is what you get. I am not trying to win a popularity contest. I am trying to be the best person I can be, to do what is required and what is right.

Perhaps the reason I am still around is because I played professional football. I realized during my first training camp that the difference between the winners and those who finish last is not the difference in talents, abilities, or techniques; the difference was who desired to be the best. I may have been lacking in the first three, but I made up for it with my desire and a fear of failure. I wanted to prove that I could compete on the highest level not only to the coaches and the other players but to myself. I wanted to find out what I was made of.

Sports are supposed to be fun and so is life. The learning experiences I got in the NFL helped me to develop my attitude, my values, my beliefs, and my moral character, which I would like to pass down to my children and their children. The reason I was cut before the first game of my rookie season is because I spent too much of my energy during training camp trying to gain the acceptance of the other players, instead of looking inside myself and attempting to reach my full potential. I decided that if I was going to be cut or fired again, it would be because I just didn't have the talent but not because of a lack of effort.

I was voted into three Pro Bowls, and that had a lot to do with playing alongside guys like Dierdorf, Banks, Young, Wortman, and Finnie. We all became better football players because we made each other better; we all knew that each of us was going to put forth as much effort as the next guy, that their desire to win was as important to them as it was to the rest of us. Do you know how it feels to walk onto a field with four other guys and know you're the best there is and that no one can beat you? Why do you think Jim Hart, our quarterback who's now in his sixties, still looks like he's 21? Because we protected him.

Looking back, a great lesson was learned: choose your partners, and your friends, carefully. You will become like them; you will live or die together. We all hung out with each other, we had the same values and the same attitude about the game, and we all knew what it took to become successful. If you hang out with coworkers at the water cooler who avoid their responsibilities and bitch about everything that is wrong with their lives, you will develop those same negative thoughts and attitudes.

What my father said is so true: "Show me your friends and I'll tell you who you are." In people's minds, you are who they perceive you to be. The closely coordinated and precise execution demonstrated by that St. Louis offensive line was as close to perfection as you can get. That's what a team is all about, that's what a family is all about, and that's what life is all about. When you find that perfect mix of personalities, work habits, and attitudes, it's a thing of beauty. Have you ever heard someone say, "Thank God for the losers, because without the losers there would be no winners"? Well, you know who said that? A loser.

I've had my 15 minutes of fame in life; sometimes I handled myself well, and other times, I am embarrassed to say, I performed very badly. I've had to deal with a massive amount of rejection, frustration, and financial pressure, and I've also had to fight the habit of falling into complacency. But I never quit. We all have a journey to make through life. It's how we handle our journey that will determine the amount of satisfaction we will derive from our trip. My journey has had its ups and downs thus far, but I can honestly say I've been blessed for the experience, adventure, and the knowledge I've learned and gained. I also like to think that I have given back to the world by taking care of my family, doing charitable work, and now by sharing what I have learned to bring awareness to NFL player disabilities and spinal cord injuries.

I suppose I have never really considered the challenges I faced to be problems. They certainly have been irritating at times, but I have tended to look at life's difficulties as opportunities to learn and grow. It is natural to make mistakes and experience failure, but we all must realize that it is normal to try, to fail, to adjust, and to try again; to learn a lesson and move forward. That's why sports have a halftime: to give the teams a chance to reconsider their direction.

There are three types of people in this world: those that make things happen, those that watch things happen, and those that wonder what the hell happened. I am one of those who make things happen. You have the choice to belong to whichever group you desire, because in the end your happiness and success in life are determined by only one thing: you. Only you can truly judge yourself and determine your course, not your parents, the economy, the government, your friends, your business associates, or your family. Your happiness at any given moment will always be your choice. The Declaration of Independence says that "all men are created equal," but it should have said "all men are created with an equal opportunity to become unequal."

After my wife's injury, I felt like I needed to get off my ass and try to make a positive impact. I wanted to learn everything I could about spinal cord injuries. I made calls, read everything I could get my hands on, and got up to speed on the latest procedures and research. I feel as if I could do my residency in neurology. My wife and I became experts on the science of stem cell research. I visited a lab and watched rats have their spinal cords broken, then witnessed the rats injected with stem cells and back on their feet three or four weeks later.

We've got plenty of walking rats already; what we need to do now is to help humans with spinal cord injuries. I get a little angry when government funding is not allocated to this cause. The faster this research can progress, the faster we can make tremendous improvements on so many people's lives. Anyone suffering from any neurological disease will benefit from this stem cell research. Forget about the Catholic Church, forget about President George W. Bush, and let's start concentrating on improving the quality of life for so many people, suffering from a host of diseases and injuries, who need this science. I believe that if God didn't want us to discover atomic energy, he wouldn't have given us the ability and knowledge to figure it out. Now that we have discovered nuclear power, the human race must demonstrate that we can use it wisely. It is a test of our moral character. The same holds true for stem cell research. With this knowledge, the human race can achieve a better quality of life for many. How far along could this research have advanced if President

Bush didn't put a hold on federal funding for stem cell research? Would he have made the same decision if one of his daughters had suffered a spinal cord injury?

As I was writing this book, I had the opportunity to recharge my batteries a little and to refocus my priorities on the present and not on the past. This book has been an internal journey that forced me to answer some difficult questions about my past and my outlook for the future. Would I stay with Joy if I won the lottery? One needs to dig deep to find an honest answer to that question. I know that by winning the lottery I would be able to provide the best opportunity for Joy to become successful in her quest to find the cure for spinal cord injuries and place her on the path to full recovery. Would I remain faithfully by her side, or would I return to those days when I had bought into my gladiator persona? How am I going to react if I go bankrupt again? Am I going to crawl into a hole and give up? I know I am not made that way.

I would like to be able to relax and not have all these different plates spinning, whether it be the credit card companies, the IRS, Joy's injuries, the NFLPA, my NFL pension, my knees, our business, or worrying about all my children finding jobs. It would be nice to get to a place where I could stop for a few minutes and just exhale.

I would like to get up in the morning and have my biggest decision be what pair of shorts I'm going to put on and what T-shirt goes the best with them. I would like to be able to sit on my front porch and tell kids to "Get the fuck off my lawn." (Even if no one is on the lawn, I'd do it just to let the neighborhood know where I stood on the subject.) I would probably get bored, but then I would be able to do exactly what I *wanted* to do and not what I *had* to do.

What is it that I want to do? I would really like to be able to share my experiences with people. I'd like to be able to go out there and tell people about my trials and tribulations and to actually leave a mark and let them know that I've been through these things and I'm still here fighting and I am doing okay, so no matter how down you get you have to keep fighting. You can bounce back and learn from your mistakes. We had an old saying in football: why would you keep doing the same thing over and over again that didn't work and expect different results? I was told that Albert Einstein said that. Well, I am no Einstein, though now my hair looks more and more like his.

What's on the horizon for my wife, my children, and me? To make predictions about the future is a difficult task at best. I may fear the unknown, but sometimes what I know about the future scares the hell out of me. What would I like the future to look like for both Joy and me? The options have been narrowed with my wife's condition, my deteriorating physical condition, and with the economy. My six kids are certainly going to have to move to different parts of the country just to find employment. It would be nice if they could all stay in the same area so I could enjoy more time with them and with my grandchildren.

For Joy and I to jump in a car or van and drive 500 miles to visit someone is a very difficult task for both of us. The daily therapy that Joy must endure just to be moderately free of pain for most of the day doesn't give us much time to chase the enjoyment that life has to offer. I would like to be able to relieve my mind of the pressure of keeping all the plates spinning so I could spend more time developing a healthy body and mind. Maybe I can't walk as well as I used to, but I can do something about my heart and I can do something about my mind. I would like to keep myself healthy so I can help Joy reach her goal of walking again someday. I have to stay healthy and stay alive in order to work with her.

I'm not a scientist. Let the scientists do their part, and I'll dedicate myself to working with Joy on the physical side of it to see what we can achieve through kinesiology, physical therapy, and working out. I would like to get her walking if for no other reason than because that doctor said she would never walk again. I would like to prove that doctor wrong, so that he will never again be able to tell another spinal cord patient that they will never be able to walk.

I want to be there to always remind Joy that God didn't create the world in one day. Life requires both patience and persistence. It is perseverance that wins races, not impatience. It's like the Alcoholics Anonymous people say: you have to take things one day at a time. Every day, every thought, every wish, and every step will bring you closer to success. I would like to be there to remind Joy every day that her progress is measured in inches, to be happy with every little gain, and to keep moving. Those inches will add up to yards and miles eventually, I am sure. I'd like to be able to work with Joy for four or five hours each day, as her therapist, to get her walking again.

That is what I would really like to do with the rest of my life. That would bring the fun back into my life. That would be a job that I love. It would be a wonderful thing. Will Joy ever walk again? Ask her. She has a very strong opinion on that. Whatever happens, I know it will be a hell of a fight to the very end, and I would like to help her win this fight. Every day would be a blessing to me, because I would be doing something of real importance to help her.

But the reality of the situation is that I have to keep working to keep our health insurance. I have to keep working to pay the IRS. I have to keep working to pay for Joy's home care. I have to keep working to pay off the mortgage. I have to keep working to pay off all of the medical bills. I have to keep working to keep my mind sharp. I have to keep working because that's all I know how to do.

I have always fought hard for victory. I am still fighting, and I am just going to keep on fighting. I'm not going to be one of those guys sitting on the couch and flipping through the channels. Remember, living is giving, and I want to actually do something positive with the little bit of time that I have left.

So often, we lose sight of what is truly important in life. I know I did. But I learned from my mistakes. You have to stop and ask yourself what is important in your life. Figure out what it is that will make you happy, not in a selfish sense or to the detriment of others, but exactly what you need to do to give you inner peace, so that you will like yourself and so that at the end of your life you will look back with pride, knowing that you did the best you could, were good to yourself, and helped some others along the way.

I have learned that your health is the most important commodity you possess, so spend some time on it. In order for you to develop the attitudes necessary for your growth, you need the energy to follow through on your plan for the future. Most of us spend more time making sure our car is running perfectly than we do on our own body. Remember that your body is the thing that drives the car. We take so many things for granted until we lose them.

The most important thing in my life is winning: as a family, father, husband, brother, son, friend, and businessman. I may come up short sometimes, but I will not allow that to diminish my desire to succeed and win. Life is not a question of this or that but rather this *and* that. There will always be good times and bad times, ups and downs. You have to take the good with the bad and keep fighting.

It is my hope that my children and those around me will profit from my experiences and will take something positive from my family's story. Sure they can take the negative. They can formulate their own opinions, but maybe when it's all said and done they'll say, "Yeah, he was an ass-hole, but in the end he was a pretty good guy."

I would like to leave you with some words that I try to live by. Some of these thoughts are mine, and some are ideas I have picked up from others:

- I've learned there is a reason God gave us two ears and only one mouth.

- I've learned that I should have spent more time with my father, to have been able to tell him I loved him one more time before he died.

- I've learned that money can't buy success, friends, or class.

- I've learned that a crowded elevator must smell differently to a midget, but he must endure to get where he needs to go.

- I've learned to live in a world of reality and not a world of "ought-to-be."

- I've learned that a successful man is not one that can make more money than his wife can spend.

- I've learned that everyone wants to live on top of the mountain, but all the happiness and growth occurs while you're climbing it.

- I've learned that there is just as much beauty in the valley if you will just stop, open your eyes, and recognize it.

- I've learned that the less time I have to work with, the more things I can get done.

- I've learned that there is no better feeling than when your little grand-child grabs your hand and says, "Come, Papa C and look at this."

- I've learned that the sweet smell of your newborn baby is the best smell you will ever experience.

- I've learned to manage to my benefit the frustrations, rejections, and financial pressures that life will inevitably throw at you.

- I've learned not to let life interfere with your life.

- I've learned that a child falling asleep in your arms is the most peace-ful feeling in the world.

- I've learned that the best way to remember your wife's birthday is to forget it once.

- I've learned to always fight fair with your wife, children, family, and friends; no one wins with name calling.

- I've learned that you can only run halfway into the woods, because at that point you would be running out of the woods again.

- I've learned that sometimes you must turn loose of the anchor and save yourself from sinking to the bottom of the sea with it.

- I've learned that just maybe I was the smartest kid in the dumbest role.

- I've learned to treat people fairly, but not equally, because no one performs equally.

- I've learned that sometimes in life the hardest choice is deciding which bridges to cross and which ones to burn.

- I've learned that often a person can meet his destiny on the road he took to avoid it and that even on the wrong road, you can find your destiny.

- I've learned that we cannot control the different things life may throw at us.

I have also learned to take everything life has to offer, to not fear failure, to continue on my journey, and to do the right thing. It's not only good for those you work and live with; it's good for you. The future belongs to those who will listen, learn, and understand that goals without action are only dreams; to realize your dreams you must put them in action. So go out and buy yourself a lottery ticket.

Shakespeare wrote that "sweet are the uses of adversity." Trust me, adversity is not always that sweet, but with the proper values, attitudes, and beliefs, the uses we make of the lessons learned from adversity can become a powerful vehicle to help us through the journey that is life.

My family's journey is not at the end of the rainbow yet; we are just near the end of the storm. I know and believe that after every storm a rainbow will appear. I hope that everyone will find their own rainbow and the courage to appreciate it when it appears. Every story has an end, but in life every ending is another beginning. So I wish you all a happy ending and the wisdom to open your eyes and find it now. Most of all I would advise this for your journey: remember to always pack an extra chin strap.

AFTERWORD

"It is not easy opening up publicly,
as I am a very private person,
but if only one person is helped
by hearing from me or Conrad
or by us opening up our lives,
then it's worth it."

Conrad and I met in May of 1985 in New Orleans. I felt that it was love at first sight. By October of 1985, I had sold my house in Louisiana, packed up my belongings and my three-year-old son Franco, and moved to Greeley, Colorado, to be with Conrad. We ended up getting married on February 20, 1988, and we have been married for 21 years. While there were some real challenges early on, eventually we got through them, and life was great. Things were really rolling for us.

By the mid-1990s we had a beautiful home, healthy children all in private schools, and a successful business. We basically had the world by the tail. We had everything we needed and then some. It had not been easy; we had to work hard to get where we were. By 2001, we had a lot of "plates spinning," as Conrad says, and then, starting with my injury, things kind of just started crashing down all around us.

On July 4, 2001, we had spent the day in the pool with the kids at our house, playing volleyball, grilling, just a typical Fourth of July day for a family. We had a couple of friends over, Larry Hall and his girlfriend, and they were both lying in our large hammock. My son Stephen, who was 12 at the time, and I were being playful and we decided we were going to jump into the hammock with them. I went first and in an instant the hammock just flipped and we all hit the grass. Fortunately our friends were not hurt, but I hit the ground hard and snapped my neck.

As a trained nurse with a lot of experience, I knew immediately that I had broken my neck; I heard and felt the snap. I could not feel my feet at all. Everyone tried to comfort me and also tried to convince me that it was only a stinger, but I knew better. As a nurse, the only thing I was thinking was, *Don't move me. Please don't move me and cause additional damage.* I admit that lying on the ground, the thought of never being able to walk again did cross my mind.

The ambulance came, and we all ended up in the emergency room at the closest hospital, which was St. Joseph's Health Center. Unfortunately, just as I had suspected, the moment I hit the ground I broke two vertebrae. The doctors diagnosed me with a fracture in my C-5 and C-6 (fifth and sixth cervical) vertebrae. They told me at the hospital I would never walk again, that I would forever be confined to a wheelchair. In a split second, I had become a quadriplegic.

I was thinking, *This is impossible.* With all the new medical advances and new therapeutic equipment, becoming a quadriplegic never entered my mind. I had a high school girlfriend who was in a terrible car accident and broke her neck, and she recovered and is walking now. Why can't the same be true for me? Sure I was scared to death, but I guess I am just not the kind of person that will allow a broken neck to keep me down. I had the same mentality of never quitting that Conrad has, and I knew I could prove those doctors wrong. I believe when the doctor said I would never walk again it was more upsetting to Conrad than it was to me, because I knew that he must be wrong. I remain convinced that I will walk again.

I spent nine months in St. Louis between Barnes-Jewish Hospital and the Rehab Institute of St. Louis, where Dr. John McDonald had his research facility. When I returned to Kansas City, the rehab facility focused on living life as an invalid, and after three months the insurance company decided to cut our coverage. We ended up going with a rehab facility in San Diego called Project Walk which is internationally recognized as a pioneer in exercise-based recovery for spinal cord injuries.

Conrad promised me that he would sell everything that we owned to finance my rehabilitation. I had concerns about the cost, but Conrad justified it by saying, "That is why we worked so hard—in order to have the money to provide for our family." All the different investments we had made were just material things and were not necessary in our life. I was also concerned about how Conrad was going to handle all the different issues he was now faced with: making sure the kids did their homework, cleaning the house, managing the business, going to PTA meetings, traveling back and forth to see me and to encourage me during my rehabilitation, and so on. He assured me he could handle it and that I just needed to concentrate on my rehabilitation.

When I first met Conrad, he was a very happy guy and full of energy, both mentally and physically. He was just full of life. He always had a smile on his face. He'll tell you, "I'm just a shy guy." I wouldn't say he's shy. I'd say he's insecure, so consequently he compensates—or overcompensates—by being the center of attention, but he was always very gracious. He would give you the shirt off his back. He is really just a big teddy bear.

When we first met he was still playing golf and skiing and was very active. Since then, I can't count how many surgeries he's been forced to endure. It is at least a dozen or more. He can barely walk now on his own; he needs to use a cane and has difficulty going up and down stairs. But he just takes pain medications and keeps going. Conrad never quits; he is a real workhorse. He is now facing another knee replacement. He almost died after his last one, and now we're scared to death. He could get an MRSA infection again, and they've already told us the odds of it happening again are very high.

To try and get rid of the MRSA, he was taking Vancomycin, a very strong antibiotic. He was in and out of the ER I don't know how many times. They performed surgery on him five different times before they could replace the hardware in his knee.

Vancomycin is only used as a last resort because it can have a lot of bad side effects, including localized pain and impairment of kidney functions. We were worried about his kidneys shutting down or that he would have liver failure, either of which could have been fatal. On top of all that, he was also taking other narcotics for the pain in his knees. We began to count his pain pills and hide them from him, because he would forget if he had taken his meds and I was afraid he was going to overdose. He was in so much pain; they were trying to just keep him down with a cocktail of Oxycontin, Oxycodone, Valium, and a host of other medications.

I am also scared that they'll come out of the surgery and tell me, "There's not enough bone, Joy." Then I'll have to make a decision while he is under anesthesia. I will have to make that call. I will have to give the doctors the go-ahead to amputate his leg. I am angry that he is in this situation and that I may have to make that decision. It's painful to watch, but we try to joke about it. You have to keep your sense of humor, especially when things are really bleak. We've joked about not having a good leg between the two of us, and about us being "the Disabled Doblers."

I'm pissed off because my husband should not have to be going through this, and he certainly should not have to be worrying about how to pay for it. I am really angry because he certainly deserves to be getting the support from the NFL Players Association to make this as painless as possible for him and to provide the support that many other retired players who are better off than Conrad receive. Those few who have been able to receive disability benefits from the NFL likely got them because of their connections to someone on the board. If Conrad was a Hall of Fame player, then perhaps the publicity would help him get the support he deserves—maybe. But a lot of highly recognized players are denied benefits, too. Without players like Conrad, a lot of those players who are in the Hall of Fame wouldn't be there.

Conrad has been turned down by the NFL and NFLPA multiple times for disability coverage and to this day has received no significant aid or support from them. He has had to wage years of legal battles which have drained him of energy and financial resources and robbed us of the precious time we have together. But Conrad will not give up the fight; if not for himself, he does it for his NFL brothers who may need help. I don't understand how he has the strength to continue the fight for himself and all the other retired players, but he really cares about the larger issues. He cares about his brothers.

It's not that the benefits or financial aid are going to make Conrad's knees 100 percent again or lessen the risk and the danger he is facing, but here's a man who is worried about how he's going to come up with the $2,000 insurance deductible he needs for this much-needed surgery. Where is the NFL? Where is the NFLPA? Phil Mickelson stepped up when he found out about our situation; the NFL has not. Not the Cardinals, not Bill Bidwell, not the Buffalo Bills. No owners, no union, no league. Not a single one. And very few current players have done or said anything. It is disappointing, but not surprising. They just don't care. Dealing with trying to get benefits from the NFLPA is just one more dragon that Conrad has to slay, one more issue that takes a piece of him away from us or that has destroyed a piece of him. He doesn't have much left. The best of Conrad has been taken and just smashed. But he keeps fighting.

After each one of Conrad's surgeries he has physically deteriorated, and certainly that has affected his personality. It's been devastating for him. For a man who's been very independent, robust, athletic, and competitive, having to swallow his pride has not been easy on him. Conrad took his job very seriously on the field. He played with a chip on his shoulder, but he had a job to do and he did it, even if it meant leg whipping or biting or stepping on people's heads. More than talent, I think Conrad has *chutzpah*. He has the heart. He has the desire. His determination to succeed makes him a winner. His teammates have told me he made them better by playing with courage and determination on every play, even when he was in pain.

He has learned about all the things that you perhaps take for granted in a relationship. You know, what does your spouse do all day? Since I have been injured, he has realized what I did all day. He has a new appreciation for single parents.

Off the field, he is that big gentle bear. But with the constant pain, his physical limitations, and all of the drugs and pain medication, his personality can sometimes take a turn for the worse. There are a lot of mood swings, a lot of ups and downs, literally, because of all the chemicals. He works hard to control it, but sometimes the drugs control him.

When the children were very young it was kind of a running joke; the children would say, "Let's get Dad some medicine, and then everybody just keep moving until the medicine kicks in." When Conrad is in that state, no one can do anything to please him. He's angry, he's hurting, and he's unaware of what he's doing to those around him. It's been very difficult to protect the children, to try and explain to them that "Daddy didn't mean that, he loves you very much." All the while, we remain very concerned about his addiction to the pain medications, and wonder, "Is this something we're going to have to live with the rest of our lives?" To this day, we're still living with it.

I know Conrad is truly in a lot of pain, but he does not talk about it. It's a way of life for him now. While many people get up in the morning and take their vitamins, he reaches for pain pills. Sure, he needs them for the incredible pain, but these are highly addictive narcotics, and I am sure that he is physically addicted to the pain pills, in addition to their ability to help him get through the day.

I think of what Conrad must feel like when he gets up in the morning. I would compare it to an angel having to get up and go to hell every day. He absolutely hates it, but he is still fighting with the business. I would say he is fighting a losing battle, but he doesn't know how to throw in the towel. Conrad refuses to quit. He refuses to admit defeat, and shutting our business down would be admitting defeat. Plus, there is the issue of our health insurance. How are we going to continue to pay the $2,400 each month for our health insurance? If we drop this policy, will we ever be able to get another one? This is why he keeps fighting to keep the business going; if it goes down, I would lose my health insurance.

Today we don't have any assets; we have been picked clean and are living hand to mouth. Fortunately we're blessed in many ways and we focus on our blessings to keep going. I'm blessed to have children and a husband that, if my help doesn't show up, will get me out of bed, dress me, and care for me. What are my options? I would be put in a public, state-run nursing home. That's where I'd be. That's where you go. What do you do if you don't have family?

I don't think I could find or hope to have ever had a better group of children. I have watched them grow up to become unselfish, apprecia-tive, giving, and unconditionally loving. They would have to be to love us, because right now and for many years, they have had to care for their parents. Conrad and I are young, really. Since they were babies, my children have been waiting on and caring for Conrad to help with his physical challenges. Stephen had just turned 12 when I had my accident. I have a remarkable group of kids and they have learned how to show unconditional love. We are truly blessed to have them as our children.

We have seen both sides of the coin. There was a time when I never even checked the balance of my checking account. If I had checks, that meant I had money. I never thought twice about buying anything or giv-ing people money and helping others. If someone needed help, we would just give them a thousand dollars and say "Here you go, pay us back if you can. If you can't, that's fine." We've seen that side, and now we're see-ing the other. We have no savings, as we gave it all up for my recovery. The pendulum has swung for us.

To be on the other side is very humbling and humiliating. I have been a Phil Mickelson, but now I'm a Joy Dobler. There are a lot of people out there who need help, and that is why we continue to give back as much as we can; we've always been very grateful for everything that we've had and that won't change. It's tough to be Joy Dobler these days but I feel blessed. I have a lot to be thankful for. I'm alive. I get to see all the kids grow up. It could be worse. I could have died. I could be living in a card-board box. I could be in a nursing home. You have to find the good in any situation. And I'm confident that it's going to get better.

It is not easy opening up publicly, as I am a very private person, but if only one person is helped by hearing from me or Conrad or by us open-ing up our lives, then it's worth it. I would prefer not to have to do it. I would prefer not to have the world know the intimate details of our life, or that Phil Mickelson paid for my children's tuition, but I think it's great that people know that there are people like Phil out there.

I have adjusted because I've made it about something bigger than me. It's not about me. It's about all the people out there who may need help and figuring out how we can help them. Right now Conrad and I can't help them with money, but if we can help them with our time, our words, our experiences, and the story of our personal tragedies, then it's worth it to have opened our lives to the public. I do a lot of public speaking and now work with the Kennedy Krieger Institute raising funds for spinal cord research. I spend a lot of time on the phone with a lot of families. The spi-nal cord injury community is very small; people hear about other people through word of mouth. I talk to you. You talk to somebody else. You find out about someone's child that has a spinal cord injury. You call them and they call you. I followed Dr. John McDonald and Dr. Cristina Sadowsky, who was my attending neurologist there. They are two of the finest physi-cians that I have ever met. I feel that they saved my life, and because of that I can now give back. I feel a responsibility to give back, and it makes me feel good to help others.

Until recently, stem cell research has been completely dependent on private funding simply because the federal government was totally against any type of assistance or federal funding. Now we are all very excited about President Obama and his support for spinal cord injury research, because the funding will definitely expedite things. Even Conrad, who is a staunch Republican, voted for Obama because of this one issue.

We lost eight years due to the Bush administration. That's just the bottom line. In spite of that, the research has moved forward rapidly. One of the biggest advances in the last four or five years has been the increase in collaboration. Things used to be held close to the vest. No one wanted to share anything, and I think they finally all agreed that it doesn't really matter who gets to the finish line first. Let's just get to the finish line, and let's all work together.

The use of embryonic stem cells remains very controversial, and there are a lot of scientists that believe embryonic stem cells remain the best option for the future treatment of spinal cord injuries. But some scientists are now looking into treatment options that don't use embryonic stem cells at all. Advanced trials are taking place on primates who have the anatomical-skeletal structure most similar to humans. In many labs, including Dr. McDonald's, they are taking the primates' skin cells, culturing them, and then creating stem cells from those skin cells. They inject those cells at the site of the injury, and the cells have been "tricked" to function as a neuron at the site, just as an embryonic stem cell would. These cells fill in the missing neural pathways; they build a neural bridge, and then the signals can cross from the brain through the spine and help build the new nerve paths necessary to control specific functions of the body. With stem cell science, the cure for my spinal cord injury could one day be an outpatient procedure; they'll take some skin scrapings from me, culture my cells, and then they'll give me a dose locally.

It is critical that the general public realizes why funding for spinal cord research is so important. Some people may say, "Well, there's only half a million of you out there." It's really not a big number. What people need to understand is that using stem cell research to find a cure for spinal cord injuries would be the tip of the iceberg for a host of other diseases: diabetes, Parkinson's, Alzheimer's, and many others. I encourage everyone to consider donating to spinal cord research and to stop for just a brief moment and think about how many lives would be improved and how many billions of dollars would be saved in the health care industry. The cost of a lifetime care plan for me, an average spinal cord injury victim, is easily over $1 million, and that's without any major complications. That's just to keep me breathing. Unfortunately, insurance refuses to pay for most of the equipment that I need to stay healthy.

Most people who have spinal cord injuries don't die from them; they die because of complications. Christopher Reeve didn't die of a spinal cord injury, he died from an infection. And why did that happen? Because he didn't have the therapy we are so close to having though stem cell science. Christopher Reeve, obviously, had access to more private resources than most people. But it was not his insurance that came to his aid. Robin Williams paid for a lot of Christopher Reeve's care, not his insurance company. Unfortunately, not everybody has a Robin Williams or a Phil Mickelson to come to their rescue.

I'm hopeful that with Dr. John McDonald's research progressing as rapidly as it is that I may be able to have surgery in the very near future and get the hell out of this chair. That's the game plan. I want to dump these wheels. They just don't match my purse and they don't match my attire. It's time to ditch them. Plus, I want to be able to stand with both feet firmly on the Senate floor in Washington, D.C., and say thank you on behalf of the 500,000 people with spinal cord injuries that will have a better quality of life and the millions more who suffer from other afflictions who will now have a chance for a better life.

What the Dobler family has now is hope, because that's all we've got. It comes from faith. I believe that bad things happen to good people, but I believe that good people can make great things happen. What we have all learned from the adversity we have had to face is to appreciate the small things in each other and realize how important family is. We have each other. We work hard to stick together. That's our commitment to each other. Going through this with my family will help them look upon every day of health as a gift.

I have had my own share of demons to work through and still struggle with them today. I am not happy about being in a wheelchair, and at times I can only vent to Conrad. I am not happy about not being the wife he married, and I find myself depressed and angry at the situation and constantly ask the same question: what if I hadn't tried to get in the hammock? But it is what it is, and I must try to find the inner strength and peace that will keep me focused on the challenges ahead. I feel a sense of responsibility in that regard; I feel that a lot of other people in my situation are depending on me to lead the way.

I also think a lot of the problems we have in the world today can be addressed by family, integrity, and sticking together. I think if people would spend more time with their families, a lot of our problems would be solved. So for the Doblers, *family* and *friends* are the key words. I think it's the answer. It's our answer.

—*Joy Dobler*

ACKNOWLEDGMENTS

Thanks to Ross Bernstein, who brought this project to Triumph Books—without your help this book would not have been possible. Co-writers and project managers Jennifer Smith and George Nugent: thank you for your contribution and dedication to me and my family.

I am also especially grateful to the following folks for their loving and generous contributions to the production of this book and to me and my family: Phil and Amy Mickelson and Glenn Cohen, I am eternally grateful for your love, friendship, and generous support of my children's educational opportunities; Dan Dierdorf, who could not be more of a brother to me—we're so close, I still can't figure out to this day why Coach Hanifan liked you best!; Michael and Maggie Garozzo and Keith and Bonnie Connell, who helped out so much with the very successful fund-raising party—we could not have made it this far without you; Gene and Marty Bicknell, for your generous financial support; Chuck Peters, whose remodeling contributions assured that our housing was always accessible and comfortable; Paul Somerville and his late wife Kathy, who have helped me through so many difficult emotional times—Kathy's dramatic fight to survive has motivated and inspired me and Joy to keep fighting; Dr. John McDonald and Dr. Cristina Sadowsky, who have taken such good care of Joy and who are global leaders in the exploration of the potential of stem cell science; Dr. Doug McDonald, for working so hard to keep me walking; Dr. Stephen Brown and Marty Gray, for saving my life from the MRSA infection; my dear friends and colleagues Jim Hanifan, Dick Butkus, George Brett, Phil Villapiano, David Humm, Keith Wortman, Larry Stewart, Carl Peterson, Mike Ditka, Marty Schottenheimer, Steve Palermo, Ginny Condon, Kelly Gerken, and Pam LaFlamme, for being there when we needed you; Don Meloni at Clear-Choice, for fixing my teeth and putting the bark back in my bite; "the Sod Sisters," Kathy McCaffrey, Cathy Hopfinger, Mo Haake, and Debbie Dreiling; "the Christmas Elves," (Head Elf) Nancy Connell, Jean Donaldson, Leeanne Orscheln, Patty Waris, Joy Cohen, and Diane Barton; Glenn and Nona Van Cleve; all the kids at St. Thomas More Catholic School, and the entire community of St. Thomas More Catholic Church; and Corrine, Chris, Clifford, Cathy, Casey, and my mother Clara.

You are all very special people, and my family and I thank you for your help and your random acts of kindness. Let's continue to pay to forward.